Higher Ground

Higher Ground

by

Janice E.M. Kolb

Blue Dolphin Publishing

Published by Blue Dolphin Publishing, Inc.
P.O. Box 8, Nevada City, CA 95959
Orders: 1-800-643-0765
Web: www.bluedolphinpublishing.com
ISBN: 1-57733-071-4

All illustrations and photographs are
by the author and/or Bob Kolb.
Cover photo by Bob Kolb.

Library of Congress Cataloging-in-Publication Data

Kolb, Janice E.M.
    Higher ground / by Janice E.M. Kolb.
        p. cm.
    Originally published: Hanover, Mass. : Christopher
    Pub. House, c 1991.
    ISBN 1-57733-071-4
    1. Kolb, Janice E. M. 2. Retreats—Miscellanea. I. Title.

BF1997.K65 A3 2000c
269'.643—dc21
                                        00-055552

PRINTED IN THE UNITED STATES OF AMERICA

This book is dedicated

to

Bob

Rochester

— My Children —

June — Laurel — Barbara

George — Jessica — Janna

and

All the "Muffins"
of
Immaculate Conception Church

"The best remedy for those who are afraid, lonely or unhappy is to go outside, somewhere where they can be quite alone with the heavens, nature, and God. Because only then does one feel that all is as it should be and that God wishes to see people happy, amidst the simple beauty of nature. As long as this exists, and it certainly always will, I know that then there will always be comfort for every sorrow, whatever the circumstances may be."

— Anne Frank
from her diary

Solitude

"I have a house where I go
When there's too many people,
I have a house where I go
Where no one can be;
I have a house where I go
Where nobody ever says "No";
Where no one says anything — so
There is no one but me."

— A.A. Milne
Now We Are Six

Introduction

"If a writer is so cautious that he never writes anything that cannot be criticized, he will never write anything that can be read. If you want to help other people, you have to make up your mind to write things that some men will condemn."

— Thomas Merton
(Trappist Monk)

Sometimes a book "just happens". It comes into being without our realizing it has been conceived and slowly matures towards its birth. This book was born in nine months following a labor of love for the One who planted the seed of inspiration within my heart to write it. In attempting to follow the deep inner desire and guidance that continually persisted in regard to my writing — I began to write a series of short stories based on actual events in the life of our family while living in New Hampshire. One of these short stories was to be about my retreat in the woods — alone in our cottage for a week. As I wrote, the story grew, for it was about situations that filled my soul. Watching the pages increase, I soon realized that what needed expressing could not be contained in the confines of a short story. As I let it flow day after day, my continuance of it was inspired greatly by our Lord — and by two people who led me on in perseverance. Each of these two persons had written an autobiographical account of a small segment of their lives — but this small segment was a powerful force that affected each of them deeply.

With these persons as models I sensed that perhaps I was being shown that I should share a segment of my life as they did, with the hope that what transpired would help others as their written accounts had helped me. I encountered only one obstacle — a very curious one — that of finding I could only write this while in New Hampshire in the surroundings where I had spent my Retreat. Therefore, there was a winter period of several months that these writings came to a standstill — though they continually were being "written" within myself with brief remembrances and ideas entered in a notebook for later expansion. They poured forth again on paper in very early Spring once back in the woods at my desk in my "room with a view" of our lake.

I thank Alice Koller, author of an exceptional chronicle, "An Unknown Woman — A Journey to Self Discovery" who gave me the courage to go away alone on my own spiritual Retreat of self discovery and healing and to keep a journal of the days. Her four months on Nantucket were the prime inspiration for my week on Lake Balch.

Ernest Hemingway also receives my gratitude for giving me his wonderful book — "A Moveable Feast" — and in it sharing not only his life in that five year period between 1921 and 1926 — but sharing so naturally and clearly his great love for writing and the disciplines he applied to his craft and vocation. A bygone era was savored anew through his writing about a young American writer in Paris and gave endless guidelines and inspiration to this new writer. To these two persons I am deeply grateful for I felt God speaking to me through their words: — "to go apart and to write it down".

I have written in a way that will tell my heart as openly as possible and yet not expose all persons and situations explicitly. Since I love in Christ all those who are spoken of in these pages, this shield of protection must exist. I pray then this loving protection will in no way interfere with the experiences I have attempted to reveal and explore.

These reflections from the daily entries made in my journal were written as an accurate accounting of all that took place that week in mind, soul and spirit. Therefore, if a certain subject appears more than once or twice or even three times — to be discussed or pondered or prayed over — it is because that is exactly what occurred while on Retreat. Matters of importance repeatedly came to mind and were written down and I have followed the journal hour by hour and day by day in order to intimately share.

Also it has been noted by my husband (and typist) and myself in the rereading and editing that my writing changed considerably as the book progressed. Tight and timid somewhat in the earlier chapters — this style disappeared and evidence of the gradual healing and strengthening the Lord was working within myself in the months following the Retreat surfaced in the freer writing of the remaining chapters.

May others hopefully now be touched and helped by the words on these pages as I was touched and helped by those who revealed their hearts' secrets and thoughts to me through the written word.

"Higher Ground"
Lake Balch
New Hampshire
September 8, 1988

Sunset on Lake Balch, New Hampshire in winter. Scene from my window.

Taken on Retreat in New Hampshire. This is the car we rented.

My husband, Bob, standing with the rented car.

Part One

"I'm nobody! Who are you? Are you — Nobody — Too?"
— Emily Dickinson

Like Thoreau — I went to the woods to be alone. Always this had been a dream — to stay by myself in our cottage in New Hampshire. Now that time had come. Depression and sadness had been settling in on me for too many months due to personal and family concerns. Each day's existence had become a hardship. My eyes filled with tears at unexpected moments. Though never intended, there were often times when I would sit for a minute to try to get myself together only to find later I had been there immobile for an extended period. Everything mattered intensely yet nothing mattered at all. The smallest chore was too big. Merely trying to begin anything was such an effort that I frequently just gave up completely. To deliberately think about the problems was painful. My feelings of utter helplessness left me questioning over and over again why I was alive and of what use was my life. I felt used and worthless — stupid and ugly. Persons I cared about and loved shocked me with their indifference and ungratefulness. Their words often stung and their behavior was frequently inexcusable. Because I loved them my pain was acute. Life was so sad and I knew that I needed help. Without morning attendance at daily Mass, which had been my spiritual joy for the past nine years — I would have fallen to pieces. It was through this Sacrament and much prayer that the inner conviction that I must go away grew stronger and could not be ignored. To go "away" meant only one place. I must go to "Higher Ground".

Just the name alone lifted my spirits. Our small green cottage and lakefront property was of such magnificent beauty to us that we lovingly named it after an old Methodist hymn we had known and sung since childhood. The selection of the name held double significance in that we drove many miles North to reach it — therefore it was "Higher Ground" in the geographical sense. But the deeper meaning of the name indicated that spiritually we experienced a closeness with God once our feet touched the earth there — and woods and water surrounded us. The chosen name carved in a piece of wood was above the side door and a large brown wooden cross was mounted on the front of the cottage above sliding doors. The cross was made by my husband — after deciding together it would be one of our "thank yous" to God who had made it possible for us to obtain this property. It was His home and the cross bore testimony to the fact and could be seen by all at great distance as they passed by in boats.

It was to this little cottage I would go. Even after the decision was made it took much encouragement from close friends to make me adhere to it. Guilt feelings about leaving family would rush through me — yet frequently I had remained at home with our family while my husband went to New Hampshire alone to make repairs in the cottage or do winterizing. Guilt it was at those times also that made me not leave when I wanted so much to go with him and have a brief respite by our lake. With all of this repeatedly pointed out to me by him and those special friends, — I had finally arrived — both in confidence and later in actually setting foot in the cottage.

But I could not simply take off as a man can. For a mother it is difficult. Courage to drive the ten hour — 400 mile trip alone was also a consideration — for that courage was missing. Then unexpected apprehension appeared in imagining being by myself in the woods at night. These were the points that came under discussion each day with my friends. Following 8 AM Mass and prayers, approximately eight to ten of us and often more — would come together at a fine little restaurant called Lena's — where it seemed all "Americana" passed through in the mornings before going separate paths into the world. It is a restaurant across the street and down a half block from our magnificent Church of the Immaculate Conception. It was in these little sessions over coffee and bran muffins served by Kathy, our caring waitress and friend, and packed into a booth meant for less persons (with chairs added to the end for late comers) — that we would help each other with individual problems, exchange books, be listeners, and always pray our Hail Mary for others intentions and our own. Due to our unchanging choice of breakfasts, Betty — who kept us light hearted and smiling with her daily witticisms — had dubbed our gradually increasing group ''The Muffins''.

Noticing all was not well, due to her spiritual discernment — my close friend Pat, sitting opposite me one morning began to delve gently into my concerns. Soon she was enthusiastically endorsing my inner conviction that I must go away. She too, had experienced a period such as I was going through and when she was given a surge of inner strength she ''ran away'' alone to her shore home by the sea to work things out in her heart that were causing pain — with the help of our Lord. Her week of solitude shared now and her encouragement each morning, supplemented by Dorothy's words of insight and love, at last deepened my determination and I began to plan the particulars.

Ruth also lovingly shared a beautiful experience with me that belonged forever to her daughter — who when her daughter was only in her teens and in high school had gone away on a spiritual Retreat with a group. A basic requirement of this Retreat forced her to stay alone in the dark outdoors for the first time in her life. She sent word through her mother after Ruth had told her what I was contemplating — that I should go away to the woods alone and would not regret having done so. Though she had been afraid, God gave her the necessary courage to endure the black night and she was grateful that she had participated and undergone this spiritual trial. Appreciating fully that a young woman whom I'd never met cared enough to reveal her own past fears and the wonderful outcome so that I might begin to put aside my fears and receive an inner change also, was the final sign that my time had come. It was here and it was now! Our Lord had used each of these friends and the overall loving support of all "the Muffins" to convince me to follow the path toward Higher Ground. With an endorsement from my family there was no turning back.

And so with plans made by my husband, Bob — we began the trip together in our van. He would not permit me to drive those long miles alone while in my sad state of mind and heart, having never driven them alone in the past. At journey's end he anticipated flying immediately back to Pennsylvania — leaving me with the van in New Hampshire. After depositing him at the limousine that would take him to Boston's Logan Airport I would be on my own.

When the van broke down in New Jersey due to serious electrical damage caused by heavy rain storms it was discouraging. With failing courage I suggested we turn back once we could. Bob refused. With long awaited road service coming to our aid — the van was put onto a giant lift and taken to a garage where it would remain all week on its own Retreat — getting repaired as I hoped to do. Bob and I — and Rochester my kitten confined in his little carrier now — rode in the cab of the lift with the young man who helped us. After signing our van into the garage and being driven to a large motel by our new friend so that we might rent a car to continue the trip — we realized we had experienced a four hour delay. And here we were now driving in a new white Oldsmobile Cutlass — a luxury we couldn't afford! Rochester — consistently an angel throughout all the delay and long ride remained on my lap when travelling. It was the second time in his young life he had participated in this 400 mile trip. Due to these problems the last limousine of the evening left the town of Rochester, New Hampshire without at least one intended passenger for the airport — whose efforts to board it failed for lack of time. Spending the night in our cottage and leaving very early next morning, we then made the drive comfortably back to the town and with our last goodbyes, Bob waved again from the limo as I watched it slowly wend away.

Getting back into the rented white Oldsmobile the realization of my aloneness swept over me with both excitement and fearfulness. I closed my eyes in prayer and asked for guidance throughout this week of my Retreat. Then driving in the direction of home by way of Lilac Mall I made a stop there in order to make a purchase in Walden Book Store. As I waited for the store to open — then soon entering it to buy a gift of "Walden" by Thoreau, and a blank book to be used as a journal for my son-in-law Rob's birthday and a small blank book for myself — a volume on the non-fiction shelf of "New Arrivals" at the front entrance seemed to leap out at me. The disturbing title made me understand that it was being shown to me by the One whose guidance I had sought only ten minutes earlier. The subject matter was dealing with a very personal problem and I left the store believing help would be received through this volume in the coming week. It was strange to feel such imperativeness to buy my son-in-law's gifts as my first sense of duty in the beginning of the week set aside for myself. But I sensed that the imperativeness was given in order that I might discover immediately the other book. Leaving Walden's I then purchased an inexpensive little digital watch in K-Mart for $2.97 because my father's watch on my wrist needed repairing and I was conveniently only a few yards from that store. Normally in New Hampshire we remove our watches so as not to be aware of passing hours. Time by the lake is precious but being alone now — a watch seemed a necessity. I was feeling stress and was very anxious to return to the cottage — yet there was no reason for anxiety and hurry. The more pressured world from which I'd come still governed my feelings and actions. Concern came over me that I was not getting on with what I came to do.

In the parking lot increasing panic bore down when I could not find the car. How could I have lost a car? After ten minutes of walking the rows of parked cars the word "stolen" flashed across my mind. Suddenly I realized in relief I was looking for our own white Pontiac still back in Pennsylvania and not the rented white Oldsmobile which was unfamiliar in appearance. Even after locating it — it still was a stranger.

This experience deepened my desire more than ever to get on with my beautiful day. Driving back, a stop in my church in Sanbornville was made and then on to my cottage where my little Rochester was waiting to greet me. The joy within as I began this first day of this week alone in this place that I love can not be told. To look out and see the brilliant blue of the lake and the magnificent colors of the changing foliage about the shore lines gave me exhilaration and hope that the week would be fruitful. I had made a rule for myself that I would not leave our property but once a day and that would be to go to the St. Anthony of Padua Church for daily Mass. Errands would have to be completed quickly afterwards — such as post office or store. Once home I was not to leave again unless an emergency arose. This would not be the week for searching for old books in favorite book barn and basements on Route 16 — or shopping or socializing of any sort. "To every thing there is a season, and a time to every purpose under the heaven." This was the time for my Spiritual Retreat. It had begun!

> "Give me, O indulgent Fate,
> Give me yet before I die
> A sweet but absolute retreat
> 'Mongst paths so lost, and trees so high,
> That the world may ne'er invade
> Through such windings and such shade
> My unshaken liberty"

—unknown—

Part Two

*"What drama be as pleasant absorbing as the interior one?
I understand hermits, but not people who can't understand
hermits. Hermits I understand all too well."*

— J. West

No one knew except Jesus how much I had longed to be here
and how greatly it was needed. I had a Monk-like soul that craved
solitude and all my reading had a bent in that direction. Among
others, I was influenced deeply by Thomas Merton — A Trappist
Monk — and his writings caused deep desire to enter the Catholic
Church and a Monastic cell. One desire more impossible than
the other, it was true "Miracle" then when the first had been
granted through much intense prayer over a two year span and
I became the only Catholic in our very faithful Methodist family.
Periods of solitude I had to create when I could and my own
prayer room at home was that quiet place in those times when
my presence was not needed as wife and mother of a large family.

Merton had written in his book "New Seeds of Contemplation" a passage of inspirational prose that seemed for my eyes
and soul alone. He said:

*"There should be at least one room, or some corner, where no
one will find you and disturb you or notice you. You should be
able to untether yourself from the world and set yourself free,
loosing all the fine strings and strands of tension that bind you
by sight, by sound, by thought, to the presence of other men."*

My blue and white room of prayer in my son's former bedroom
was the answer to this for me — a room I went to whenever I
could. When I couldn't be at Mass or in the darkened sanctuary
before the Tabernacle praying — or by the lake in my prayer

chair or within the cottage — then my Prayer Room met that monastic need in my soul. Bob had paneled and painted and treated me to a soft blue rug after suggesting my use of this room. My religious objects and spiritual books were overflowing throughout our home and here they could be displayed and confined to this one area. It had been blessed and dedicated to our Blessed Mother and painted her colors of blue and white, for it was her powerful intercession to our Lord through the Rosary that I knew made possible my very impossible calling to the Catholic Church to be fulfilled.

Reluctant to ask Our Lord that I might enter the Catholic Church because I felt it selfishly wrong to permit my deep inner longing to this call to be lifted in prayer — I did nothing. I was born and raised and married a Methodist and we raised our six children in the Methodist Church. It was frustrating being drawn intensely to the Eucharist daily and it seemed as if my soul was imprisoned in a strange body. I could not understand why He had placed this deepening desire within me if it was never to be realized.

Waiting one day for a red light at an intersection on *Church Road* (a significant "sign", I felt — to what followed) an inner voice spoke clearly and directly to me instructing me to begin praying the Rosary that my dream to become a Catholic might be brought to fulfillment. It was in the month of December (1976) — Mary's month and the month of our Lord's birthday.

Purchasing a blue Rosary and using a Rosary booklet given to me by a friend — I began to pray the mysteries on the day that my father had a very serious operation in a Catholic hospital. Before me was a Crucifix on the wall of the waiting room as I stumbled through the prayers and fingered my new Rosary beads. I continued to pray daily in this way. Exactly two years later in the month of December Our Blessed Mother's intercession opened for me the doors of the Catholic Church that I might enter. My miracle had been obtained and I became a Catholic on the Feast of St. Lucy who had been given the light of faith and who promised to preserve this same light in our souls —

so that we may be devoid of the blindness and darkness of evil and of sin. She is the saint to turn to for perfect vision of our physical eyes also so that they may serve for the greater honor and glory of God and for the salvation of souls in the world. It was a night of LIGHT and GLORY that December 13th, 1978 as my reception into the Catholic Church was brought to completion.

It was an added gift that I worshipped in my parish church named for Our Blessed Mother under the title of The Immaculate Conception. It was no accident that I was received into the Catholic Church in the month of December that held her Feast Day under this same title on the 8th, and three anniversaries also of another convert — Thomas Merton. He had entered the novitiate of the Trappist Order on December 13, 1941 — the same day I was entering the church — though I did not remember this fact at the time I entered but rediscovered it in his journal at a later day. The other two anniversaries marked his entrance through the doors of the Abbey of Gethsemani on December 10, 1941 and that of his untimely and sudden death by accident — also on a December 10th in 1968. These were God-incidents in my spiritual life — not coincidences — for I believe I was truly helped from above through the heavenly Communion of Saints in the church triumphant — most especially through Mary and her devotee and my mentor — Thomas Merton — and also by my own Father and Mother and special uncle and close friend Bill who had all died in this two year interim since December 1976. I asked their help again as I turned to Jesus in prayer on this momentous first day of my Retreat. Then I changed into comfortable shirt and jeans, made myself a cup of tea in my favorite large porcelain cup covered with violets — and curled up at the end of the sofa with ''Chester'' in my lap and my new found book from Walden's in hand. The cup had been given to me by my loving friend Rose-Beth from my daily Mass ''Muffin'' circle — reminding me from 400 miles away that my morning group there was praying for me. Rose-Beth had chosen the violet floral design in memory of another Violet — my Mother — and with a square violet covered ceramic coaster to use with it.

Despite my depression and concerns that brought me to this day — the joy within was excruciating. I wanted only to stay here the rest of my life for the realization that "THIS REALIZA-TION" of aloneness was here, made me wish it would never end. It had taken so very, very long to accomplish it that I could not bear to think in terms of only one week. I wouldn't! I would savour each hour like it was golden and be like a delighted child. For I was — I was a girl in my heart and incredulous that at last I was here alone!

Thoreau has written in Walden — *"I love to be alone, I never found the companion that was so companionable as solitude"* — and Thomas Merton expresses this joy of solitude well when he writes in his journal "Sign of Jonas": *"Once God has called you to solitude, everything you touch leads you further into solitude. Everything that affects you builds you into a hermit, as long as you do not insist on doing the work yourself and building your own kind of hermitage".*

Our Lord had long ago begun His hermit-building within me — but never had I dreamed He would give me a hermitage experience in the woods to live as my friends Thoreau and Merton had. These writings would become even more alive to me now as "THIS HERMIT" began a new lap of her spiritual journey. For very long I had known this most important of solitudes — that of the solitude that one must maintain within his soul despite all that is going on about him outwardly. Now that inner solitude was permitted to be in its physical hermitage in the woods — and who could have imagined that this experience would at last be mine. Not I! Praise God for His mercy and love!

Part Three

"How many a man has dated a new era in his life from the reading of a book."

— H.D. Thoreau

I read and read while tears continuously filled my eyes and finally I could read no more. Closing the book I sat and cried until I felt drained. It just happened. There had been no forcing it. There were many wonderful books on the shelves in this cottage that I had been accumulating from library book sales at home and from old book barns and basements in nearby Ossipee, New Hampshire in order to build up our library here and there were books I brought along with me to read — but it was this newly purchased book that I knew I was to open first. Within the first several pages I knew why He had sent me to Walden's with such urgency. He wanted this in my hands the first day so that I might have light on several situations in my life that have caused deep personal anguish for many, many years. Beginning this short Retreat then with new understanding would perhaps put me in a different frame of mind and lift the depression and I could better get myself in order — or He could. The time alone then would be more beneficial than had I not discovered the book. And so to brighten myself I laid it aside and opened my new blank journal. Keeping a journal was important to me and a discipline I required of myself — though I did not always make entries on a daily basis. A nice medium sized hardback unlined book I used as a regular journal kept in my prayer room — but I also carried a small red hardback with me so that I could make spur of the moment notations about feelings, happenings, thoughts, surroundings or anything else that I didn't want to

11

lose in forgetfulness. Or perhaps in the waiting to enter it in the regular journal — IF I remembered — it might lose some of the fervor or immediacy of the moment.

Now I was beginning a third journal which would keep this week apart not only in memory but also in book form. This week was to be significant and deserved its own "place" just as I was in a place apart. And so I began to write and entered all that happened thus far from the time we left home and even to the evening before that of my husband's 40th high school reunion. I felt the reunion should be included, for aside from the lovely evening there was also an encounter with an old friend of ours whose conversation dealt with one of my own personal problems — or in part — that the new book of today was dealing with also. The conversation he surprisingly initiated specifically on this delicate situation, revealed he too had a similar problem causing him pain. I believe Jesus permitted this friend and myself to talk about this pain as a further help in my Retreat — for a high school reunion was an unlikely place for such a discussion. I prayed He helped my friend too.

Writing is always a lovely and essential release for me and just seeing the blank journal and my favorite pen provided motivation and drew me to them like a magnet. Twelve pages were filled within a short period. No food — just another cup of tea, and then more reading — but of another sort — books packed and brought along for sheer inspiration. Some made the trip for the purpose of my rereading large portions in each for encouragement, assurance, and pure joy — books I could never get enough of and never, never tire of certain passages within them. Combined they touched and fed various aspects of my nature, interests and problems. Separately there were a number of personal journals, two autobiographical accounts — each of very short segments in each author's life, and several biographies of persons I loved though had never met — but whose lives had influenced mine. Also several volumes of letters of writers and more.

I knew I couldn't read or reread all of these in this short Retreat but it is one of my many eccentricities that I MUST have as many books with me as I possibly can for I just might need one — or all! Whether it is coming to New Hampshire to stay or just going down to the water's edge in my prayer chair — never am I without a generous supply of books. They are more important than food, drink or clothes and the only things that equal them in necessity or desire are wonderful large legal pads of various colors, a handful of pencils, my journal, and my favorite pen. But always a variety of books!

Upon reading a journal of the fine author Jessamyn West earlier in this same month — a true "find" at my local library book sale before coming on this Retreat — I was pleasantly brought up short in discovering an entry in it that really made me smile and feel good inside. Revealing humorously a special quirk about herself I knew in the reading of it I had found a soul sister! Perhaps her own words describing herself are better than mine and through them you will understand us both:

"I have two dozen books with me. Stuart was taken back. 'I hope you didn't think there'd be time to read all of these,' he exclaimed — I said, 'No, I don't.' The next question — 'Why do you have them then!' — I didn't answer at once. I feel panicky — perhaps that's too strong a word — traveling without them. I don't even like to go from my room to sit on the lawn without taking a half-dozen books with me. 'It's my insurance policy,' I told him finally. 'Insurance against what? Boredom?' I don't think of it that way. Though perhaps in the back of my mind there is the conviction that as long as I have my books all other evils (beside the loss of them, I mean) will be bearable. Perhaps I am like a person who, having once endured a famine, wants always to have a supply at hand. Though I never suffered from any real famine of books. Less than I wanted, perhaps, though that still seems to be my state. I always take with me not the same books but the same variety of books. Half usually more than half, will be books I've read before. A couple of Thoreau's journals. Some poetry new or old —" and so on she confides.

Not only did that make me smile but when I read her utter love and feelings for book stores I knew I had met a fellow pilgrim as strange as myself. I doubt if I could have expressed it as completely as she but then I never had to try. Those who know me

— especially my daughters — steer me clear of them if they are with me. If their distractions fail they leave me "to be" — in the bookstore alone — with instructions to remain there. They come back later — collecting me as they would a child — after completing their shopping. It is also known their mother may be found any Saturday night when at home in Pennsylvania in our local Encore bookstore — first having had dinner at the Oaklane diner with their father. Making a visit to my church for prayer and often confession, completes my outing. I am only accompanied to dinner. Bob, who is a fellow hermit — may turn into a pumpkin if out past 7 PM on these nights. We part temporarily. This is as exciting as we wish our Saturday evenings to be for they are perfection. Then home to join him and to enjoy whatever book or books I absolutely NEEDED that very night. Always they are on sale.

The same compulsion within for library book sales exists. There are not enough shelves to hold all of my books but I am always present at the library the day of the sale. Marvelous surprises can also be found there for others. Right and left I throw the beautiful sale books in my large bags for friends or family as I come across subjects that will interest them. Any others addicted to books and bookstores will find Jessamyn West's description of her addiction rather normal — perhaps more driving than their own — but similar. She is, however, describing my own personal addiction in describing her own. She makes this entry in her journal while out of town and in a hotel room:

"I'm as drawn toward a bookstore as an alcoholic is toward a bar — only my case is really more neurotic. The alcoholic doesn't I think, with a room full of bottles, feel the need of going off in search for the one perfect bottle which has, so far, eluded him. Actually, such a compulsion might be the alcoholic's saving — as it can be the readers' undoing. The alcoholic might spend so much time searching he would have little time for drinking. Less drinking is obviously good for the alcoholic. Perhaps less reading is also good for the inebriate of print. I have been sitting here looking down on the tide of prismatic automobile tops, fighting the desire to hail a taxi and go off in search of a bookstore. If others

with my weakness had banded together for mutual aid, I might call a fellow inebriate, ask him to come sit with me, hold my hand and feed me black coffee until the longing was conquered."

And so to my reading from the selection that travelled with me. There was only one destined to be read from next.

Part Four

"I shall lead you through the loneliness — the solitude you will not understand; but it is My shortcut to your soul."
— Thomas Merton

Two years ago the reading of an autobiographical account by a woman in search of herself had left me just astounded. It was as if I were reading about myself and I was dumbfounded that another could be feeling so much of the hurt and confusion I was feeling and that she was not only able to put it into words but she had had the courage to face herself at last and to do something. From despair and near suicide she had come back to the beginning of a new life after an extended period of solitude in the dead of winter 30 miles out to sea on Nantucket Island — with a new little puppy as her only companion. She was single, with a lifestyle not even similar to my own, but psychologically and emotionally we were kindred spirits though unknown to each other. I had seen the book a number of times on shelves in various bookstores and each time lifted it out — read the remarks on the cover — and — placed it back on the shelf. One day I knew I would buy it for it was waiting there confronting me. That day came and because it did I was here in my own solitude by the lake in the woods — alone with only my new kitten. I hold Alice Koller — author of "An Unknown Woman" chiefly responsible for this Retreat and consider her my prodder and pusher and inspiration to finally come away as I had. When the tears had dried from the first reading of it I immediately began it again. There was so much in every page to be absorbed. Though I had never written to an author before, I was moved to write to this one and received a very caring and informal reply encouraging me to take time alone and also answering questions I had posed to her. Immediately after that I was able to go to New Hampshire with only my husband for one week and though it was a week of quiet and reflection and writing with no other member from our family along — it was still not the total aloneness that I needed — though very fine.

Often I had felt impressed to give this particular book to a friend. With only two exceptions — each time I had given it (and there were many) I had heard Him correctly — for each except those two who received the book needed it as I had and wrote or called to say that the book was about her life as well as Alice Koller's. I continued to read it over from time to time or to lift out passages or pages to reread for encouragement.

Now at last I was here to find within my own self and being what she had also gone apart to find. I envied her three months on Nantucket in comparison to my week on Balch Lake. But I was deeply grateful for what I at last had and yet knew it would only be the beginning of the search and sorting out for me, due to the shortness of my Retreat. Like myself she was moved by Thoreau and understood the private business he went to transact at Walden — believing it to be what she had been doing in the months of her "Walden". Thoreau states that he went to the woods and then that he left it for as good a reason as he went there. I am fairly certain that I, too, went to the woods to transact a private business similar to his — and to Alice Koller's — but unlike them I had to leave the woods reluctantly. I was not free to stay endlessly or for much longer than a week until I completed my experiment of finding answers and self and peace as they had done. My decision to leave was not made by me — but for me — due to family responsibilities. And even this fact was part of my *private business* — my inability to be *me* with my own power to make my own decisions. Not that I wished to rebel for I believed in family life and sharing and caring and coming to decisions together as a unit. But I lived as a woman directed by other person's decisions for me — whether deliberately done by them or not — and it often caused a feeling of helplessness. Perhaps the depression had made this area of my life seem more serious than it really was — but I doubted it. I also saw it as a weakness in me because I permitted it to be — and more reason to hate myself.

And in this frame of mind — though feeling joy at the same time for this time of solitude I was just entering — ''An Unknown Woman'' was opened once again to seek out the underlined passages that brought incentive and reassurance and emboldment to change myself and my life and rid myself of the despair that all too often filled me within. I simply couldn't leave these woods the same person that had arrived in them no matter how short my stay or accomplishment — or all would have been in vain. If only one step had been taken, one wrong righted, one heartache healed — then I would feel it had been at least a new beginning along a long road still to be journeyed to become whole and to know myself and my goals.

Pausing before becoming thoroughly engrossed in my reading and thoughts — I again opened my new journal to enter a quotation of Thoreau's — a quotation already entered in every other journal I had written and completed. It was a personal requisite to be at hand in each current journal so as not to have to make a search for it when it became utter necessity to my soul:

''I went to the woods because I wish to live deliberately, to front only the essential facts of life, and see if I could not learn what it had to teach, and not when it came to die, discover that I had not lived.''

I remembered as I entered it the words that made me smile from an entry in another journal — a journal that I already felt at home in though it was only a recent acquisition — the journal of that new soul sister — author Jessamyn West:

''I can copy anything I like forever. If all of Thoreau's writings were to vanish from the earth there is still enough of him copied into journals to preserve his essence for future readers. There are people who don't understand this and I don't understand it completely myself — the best analogy, I think, is that of a pianist wanting to play the music he reads.''

Why was it that her entries so frequently contained my very thoughts and spoke of very actions I too had performed? I knew, just as He had set Alice Koller's book in my sight so He had set Jessamyn West's and many books before that that had brought me along in my spiritual journey to this very point. They were put there to teach and instruct and inspire — but also to reveal — very especially in these wonderful writings of these two women — that others too, had been where I was now and yet had made it through the rain. Like Thoreau — when it came to die — I did not want to discover that I had not lived.

Part Five

The first day slowly passed in this manner — reading, reflection, writing, prayer and tears. My kitten Rochester stayed usually on my lap either sleeping or just gazing at me. Playing with my pen or sitting on my journal as I alternately lifted him to my side, wrote, lifted him, wrote — I couldn't help but laugh and hug and kiss him in his determination to be right in the middle of my journal pages. Often I would let him sit when I returned to my reading. This dear little furry "purrson" marked my place until I wrote again. Occasionally he'd leave me for a brief time and looking up I would see him sitting across the room in the kitchen sink just staring at me. It was a favorite spot of his for contemplation and I was very thankful that he was mine — this beautiful little orange and white furry kitten whose little head and neck was all that appeared above the sink. A carton and paper bag were on the floor for him to play in but he soon wore himself out and returned to my lap.

I felt he was a gift in my life — for all my married life my husband had been opposed to my having a cat. Having grown up with them I had missed one as my own. On our first trip to our cottage that same summer my daughter Janna and I encountered a man with two kittens to be given away in the Rochester, New Hampshire Mall and in a moment of weakness my husband had given in. Even he did not regret it now, for Rochester — named after the town in which God had set him down just for us and

Rochester sitting in kitchen sink.

Rochester — 4½ months.

Rochester

called "Chester" as well — had proven to be all love and no trouble. He did not even "Me-ow" — but remained silent always — using his big golden eyes to communicate and his nestling and snuggling to prove his devotion. He was contemplative and tried to show me by his silence and gentleness that he had a Monk-heart as I did. And so we two grew closer in our solitude.

Breaking the mood briefly I phoned the church rectory to inquire of the priest about a young woman who had collapsed in church two weeks ago. Our family had been praying for her and when I had called from Pennsylvania after returning there two days following her collapse — Fr. Norman had told me it was due to an aneurism in her brain and no hope was held for her recovery. Now through this second call I learned of her death two days after my first call. I sat down and wept. When a volunteer had been asked for before Mass by Fr. Norman to read the scriptures that Sunday — we saw this young woman's hand go up immediately — a woman in her early thirties with two teenagers and husband. She had freely offered herself to read the Word of God and had only read several verses when she collapsed backwards to the floor. Somehow we all sensed it was more serious than a faint. The congregation sat quietly praying for her for twenty-five minutes until a paramedic team arrived and an ambulance sped her away. Another mystery to think upon. Vibrant and alive one moment and wanting to serve — unconscious the next moment never to return as she was before to this world — to her own little world of family. Had she — if she had been given reprieve and been able to ponder only seconds — when it came to die — discover that she had not lived? Or would she have known contentment in what her life had been and been ready to meet her Lord? Yes, I was ready to die and desired it too frequently. It was the living I found painful all too often. I didn't want to be one of those many that Thoreau spoke of who live lives of quiet desperation. It gave me such happiness to give myself to others in sharing Jesus through letter writing, books, conversations, visits, and every day encounters — but inwardly the self-hate and unworthiness to even feel like I should be taking up space on this planet crowded out all the goodness of my outward Christian life. I felt like a fake — telling others the joy of the Lord, yet within I was usually barren of anything that resembled joy. Oh this hadn't always been — especially since my miracle of becoming a Catholic. This gift brought deepest joy! At Mass and in receiving Him in Communion each day I felt strength and new resolve and gave all my discouragement and despair to Him. But not long out into the world in which I dwelled I did not always live and move and have my being in Him as scripture promised we should. Yet He used me over and over again even in this sad state I was in and wretch that I was — and somehow others found Jesus in and through me or so I am told — despite the mess that was inside my being. That was hope — a thin strand of hope to hang onto — informing me when I wasn't too depressed that I could not be as worthless as I felt for He gave me His love to give and share with others. If only I could continuously feel He loved me as He loved them. I felt His presence in Communion and prayer and did not feel abandoned. Just not worthy — and ugly and awful. I knew why and yet could not be strong in righting the onslaughts in my life that would make me feel alive again and a real person. It was my own fault. As a Christian and a Catholic I had all at my disposal for a happy, joyful life. I was letting it be marred deeply and yet would not take a firm stand to stop the very reasons for causing me to live less a life than should be lived when living in Him.

On my personal phone in my prayer room at home I kept a tiny wooden plaque upon the dial to see whenever I made a call or received one. It was to brace myself for contacts — and very especially with a beloved friend. If I needed such support for calls with someone so close — how could I manage with others? The little ringed plaque that I later learned held words attributed to Eleanor Roosevelt read: *"No one can make you feel inferior without your consent."* It was my giving consent that gave me reason for this week alone — or one of the chief reasons — and one of the most difficult to comprehend. It was not only in the present of my life but had been a pattern all through it and it would continue in the future if this week did not make a difference and end this state that only brought destruction and despair to heart, soul and spirit. It included also the awfulness of the continuing situation discussed with our friend at the high school reunion and the fallout of incidents stemming from that severe problem in our home and my person. It was complex and like a giant thumb. It pressed me down into the ground — sometimes so much so that I had no will or strength to rise above it and break free. I gave in and lived a below par existence believing there was more to life but I just could not achieve it. This week had to be a turning point. Rochester and I were here alone with Jesus and He had the power to give us more than we ever hoped or desired (Ephesians 3:20). I already had the most precious miracle — that of my Catholic Church and faith — and continually praised Him and thanked Him. Always upon entering the sanctuary and down on my knees my first words in prayer were "Thank you for permitting me to be a Catholic". Now — if only I could be made to feel worthy of this high calling and to the promises of Christ. That's what this Retreat was about.

Part Six

"Man lives by affirmation even more than he does by bread."

— Victor Hugo

It was dinner time though I was not following any strict schedule. But I knew because my sweet silent Chester was sitting on the end of the table patiently waiting for his little bowl to be put down. I prepared his food and placed it before him and felt satisfied I could make his little heart happy in so many ways. It was a joy and a gift to give him joy — but nothing I did for him could ever compare to all that he gave to me to feed my mothering instincts and my heart — because I was ecstatic that Jesus had made it possible that I had at last had a kitten.

I then opened a Lean Cuisine and put it in the oven — and boiled water for tea. It was all I planned to have because though not fasting completely from all food this particular week I was eating very sparingly. I planned only one small meal a day and only tea or coffee in between with perhaps some brown rice cakes if I needed anything at all. This too, was something that needed to be dealt with and I hoped it would be at least touched on while on Retreat — that of my fear of food. It was not like smoking or drinking or drugs. Eating could not be totally pulled from your being like other things harmful — though I had certainly tried it on many occasions through the years with extremely long fasts to deepen my spiritual walk and to help achieve spiritual enlightenment while the body was free of the food that dragged it down and made it feel drowsy, slow and loggy. And I surely had diminished my desire and need for it, usually eating only one meal under normal circumstances — only occasionally two.

The majority of this discipline was truly for spiritual reasons for we are to do all for the glory of God — even our eating and drinking. But a small portion of the denial of food regularly was the fear of it and what it did to me. Slow to lose weight and morbid when I gained, I felt food — though delicious and desirable — my mortal enemy. Extremely self-conscious over even existing and walking about, if I gained even a pound I could hardly operate as a human being. I never felt good about myself and feared being heavy and therefore I wasted valuable creative time worrying about food. So I did not eat in a normal way and probably never would. That did not worry me — it was just the very bother of the stress over it. I prayed I would find some answer for this, but in the meantime I would enjoy my oriental Lean Cuisine, my wonderful hot tea and my book.

Into the woods came the ringing of the phone that first evening and not once but many times. In the silence it seemed to almost jostle the room and I ran to answer so it wouldn't continue. It was one of my daughters to check on me and cause me to laugh with her sweet silliness. Jessica — always caring and fun-loving had called me during the day also. Her call was followed by another daughter's — Janna — and that too was special. Though both lived at home they had made separate calls. I put on the tea water and answered still another ring — that of our newly married daughter Barb. Calling to see if I was safe she also wanted to express thanks for a photo album of wedding pictures I had taken of her marriage to Frank in August. My children were friends as well as daughters and son and this was a consolation that was always with me. I had six best friends forever — or so I prayed and hoped.

More tea and reading and more ringing of the phone. This time it was a blessed friend — a retired obstetrician and poet, Dr. Francis McGeary — whom I referred to as ''Friar Francis'' due to his love of Thomas Merton, his Monk-heart and his spiritually living in the Abbey of Gethsemani, Kentucky — though he really lived in my home town of Jenkintown. He had nicknamed me ''Trappistine Jan'' and phoned to see if I was happy in my hermitage in the woods as Merton had been when he lived in his. We had a wonderful conversation as always and he read me his latest spiritual poem which he had written that same day. We had met in our Immaculate Conception Church — sitting in the same back pew for years at daily Mass but never exchanging more than a "hello". One day in spirit — Thomas Merton broke the ice for us and we began to exchange conversation and poems and books and speak of our mutual love for Merton and of course, Our Lord Jesus and Our Blessed Mother. But to speak of all this longer would create another story unto itself and so I will just say his call made me laugh and also appreciate the goodness and warmth of loving spiritual friends.

Soon after, my close friend Dorothy — from my morning daily Mass and Muffin group called just to make sure I was happy and safe. She also knew and loved "Friar Francis" and was laughing that he too should call. We agreed that Merton never had such luxuries as loving phone calls while he resided in his hermitage alone on the grounds of the great Abbey of Gethsemani. But like "Trappistine Jan" — Merton wrote hundreds and hundreds of letters so I at least knew that he was fulfilled in friendship in the human form by letters from all over the world, due to his initial efforts in spreading God's love through his own letter writing. The last call was from my husband to say he had arrived home safely from his flight and so I settled down to more prayer and reading and writing in my journal.

I had come to the woods to be alone to get my life together — yet the world followed me there through these phone calls. But I couldn't be disturbed that my silence was broken into because these loved ones made me feel less depressed and that I mattered and that I couldn't be all bad as I always felt. One of the reasons I came away was because I seemed not to matter to people I loved and so almost at once the very first night alone — God brought loving family members and friends into my solitude to affirm my life and to tell me that my absence was noticeable — or at least I wanted to believe that.

Now it was dark and very much night and blackness and I drew the drapes and curtains, locked the door which is never locked during the day and settled down to my first entire night in the woods alone. I came to the woods like Thoreau to transact business and a lot of that business had to do with fear. I was filled with fears of all sorts that affected my life and pulled me down. You could attach other names to the fear, which I did — but underneath it was always fear.

I was fearful of staying alone in the woods yet I had taken this step to overcome it because I was desperate to be whole and healed. I was amazed I was this far into this fear for it was September and no one was around. Had I come in summer I would have occasional neighbors though not close by. I came with the fear in me of failure and of not having achieved anything in life but having six children and trying to raise them. I came with the fear of not ever being able to write a book or any other writings — aside from all the hundreds of letters I wrote through the years and the journals I kept. I was bursting inside with desire to write and write for Him — but never was it released. I was totally bound up and blocked. All my journals had pages of bemoaning this and my miserable state of utter uselessness. To see shelves of books in a book store and to realize each was written by a capable person and that I did not fall into that category even though the desire to write was overwhelming — actually drove me crazy — or caused frustration and depression most severe. I felt like the composer Salieri who longed for the desire to compose glorious music to the honor and glory of God and was a waiting instrument begging to be used for this marvelous purpose. Yet instead he was denied this until his dying day and the gift was given to Mozart who did not take it seriously and whose behavior lacked the grace and refinement to accompany such a gift. This caused Salieri anguish as he lived in the presence of Mozart and watched Mozart's life dissipate when he, Salieri, so ached to serve God in the composing of beautiful music. I was like Salieri indeed! I understood! I longed to write and though I begged Him to let it flow out of me — it never did except in the form of letters or those journal entries I made most regularly.

These fears took over my life even though I knew the answer was Jesus Christ. Somehow I could tell others how to "let go" but I could not appropriate this in my own life and give all to the Lord. I couldn't walk into a restaurant alone and enjoy even a cup of coffee by myself in a nice little booth. My own daughters did this. I couldn't enter a room of people alone or speak to a group. I feared betrayal also because I had been betrayed oh so horribly.

How would I conquer these fears during this Retreat or at least begin to conquer them? How many still would hold me down making me less a person? How would I deal with any future betrayal? How would I deal with depression and unworthiness? I knew the power of Our Lord Jesus and I received His body and blood daily in Holy Communion and I believed that He casteth out all fear and so in Him I would place my trust and believe with all my heart that this Retreat would indeed be a turning point and a new beginning. I prayed I could again capture the utter abandonment I had to Him in the first six years of my conversion to the Catholic faith, and again feel the excitement and unexplainable joy that would constantly be welling up inside me despite the awful problems and persecution without, due to this very conversion and entry into the church that brought me such supernatural spiritual joy.

Part Seven

"Let nothing disturb thee,
Let nothing affright thee.
All things are passing.
God never changes.
Patience gains all things.
Who has God wants nothing.
God alone suffices."
— St. Teresa of Avila

The alarm jangled waking me and the phone rang almost before I could silence the alarm. It was my husband calling before he went to the office and to see if I had had a good night and also to make sure I was up early. He knew my plans were always for daily Mass. After brief conversation I got ready for church and drove the winding Route 153 to Sanbornville as the colored foliage all about me made me so happy within. Only five others were at Mass but I knew them all from summer attendance. Our daily group was always small. Following Mass — and prayers alone — I stopped at our local grocery store and then to the Post Office. I always had outgoing mail to send home and was pleasantly surprised to find I had received a letter from my close friend who was attending a spiritual conference in Rome.

Now it was time to conquer a fear I was determined to handle here in this little town I loved and in my favorite restaurant. I slowly drove across the street, parked — and timidly went to the door of the Nest and actually walked in. Today was the day I was to enter and eat in a restaurant alone! A phrase came to mind I once embroidered on a sampler. *"Fear knocked at the door. Faith answered. No one was there."* I had answered with

33

faith by approaching the door of the restaurant and now I was in a fine red cushioned booth by a brightly red and white curtained window. My waitress was pleasant and chatty and I liked her instantly and she wasn't aware she had helped me over the threshold of fear.

Waiting for breakfast I read the letter from my friend overseas and thoroughly absorbed it by rereading it several times in order to remove myself from the restaurant surroundings temporarily. It was a pleasure to read and hear the news and it also served as a buffer for me to keep a certain solitude.

Ordering a small breakfast was all I intended in order to keep the regimen I planned of barely eating. One egg arrived, a bran muffin and coffee — delicious coffee. I had ordered the bran muffin to be in spirit with my wonderful group of friends back in Jenkintown who also had attended Mass and were now seated as always in a booth in Lena's across the street from our beautiful Immaculate Conception Church. They would all be ordering bran muffins and coffee. They knew I would be also for they knew my intention of conquering this fear. Before eating I inwardly said the "Hail Mary" as they would be doing as a group. When we silently prayed our "Hail Mary" together in Lena's the entire crowd in the delicatessen would fall silent as we prayed. They were not certain what we prayed but they surely knew that indeed we prayed. God's spirit was in our midst.

After a second cup of coffee I left the restaurant quite exhilarated within as having accomplished a very major work. However this was not a true test — for only several others were having breakfast there and how would I deal with a large crowd or a packed restaurant as it always was in the evening? I could only take one step at a time. Perhaps this was all I was ready for this week — but when confronted with a full blown crowd I would find that in my weakness He would be strong.

Back to the cottage over the rough dirt road and entering the cottage I found little Chester eagerly awaiting my return and to be cuddled. We settled down to day two of our wonderful Retreat in solitude — our Walden experience.

Though impressed that I had begun to handle fear I had been a failure the night before in this department. I was afraid at night because the little sounds outside in the dark were blown up into larger proportions in my mind and so the matter seemed serious — far more serious. I began by sitting up on the sofa — but eventually lying down on it to sleep. I left soft lights on and believed all this to be safer because the sofa seemed nearer the phone. Though we have barely any reception due to our low location by the lake I nevertheless put the television on softly so I couldn't hear outside noises. The static from the set helped me to blot out imaginings and from hearing the least twig crack outdoors. In my fear I at least had the sense to realize I would misinterpret any noise and so provided these coverups for myself. I really was a failure with no faith or trust in this particular area, yet all women I spoke to afterwards said they could not have stayed there alone as I did. It was not a fair assessment however because some of these friends had never seen our cottage and perhaps they would have been braver if they had been more familiar with the surroundings or it had been their home. I can say that I still was not putting my fears — or certainly not this one — in our Lord's hands or trusting implicitly but I felt He understood and was probably smiling at my idiosyncrasies and waiting for me to turn myself and the fear over to him completely. He was patient. The Holy Spirit is a gentleman — never pushing — and so He was waiting for me to be more open and willing for Him to enter and lead me in His power through my fear and into my total healing.

Having given this enough time in my thoughts I turned now to the book I had begun to read that I had bought the day before. It was as if the author knew me personally and that she was writing about my life. She knew what I had experienced because she had also — and as a psychiatrist had helped other women — no, many women — with this very same problem. The tears poured out again and I sat and read until I again could see no more. Wiping and reading I continued until my eyes felt worn with the flow. I knew He had wanted this book for me this very

Retreat because my past had an effect on my present and so many of the problems I was trying to deal with this very week stemmed from the problems of the past — most especially this one. It was overpowering.

After my cup of tea was made I put that book aside to read from other books that would give me insight into other hearts. Perhaps as often happened when I read other writer's journals I would find solutions for my own concerns and see joys that were like mine or see sweet secrets from another soul to mull over all the day long and feeling that author's presence to me in a new way because he had told me this sweet confidence.

I gathered about me some of my favorites including Thoreau's, Jessamyn West's, Katherine Mansfield's, Anne Morrow Lindbergh's and Thomas Merton's "Sign of Jonas" — the journal he kept in those first early years as a new Trappist Monk. This journal in particular had me even more on fire for the Holy Eucharist and the Catholic church when I discoverd and read it many years ago as a Protestant. His journal entries were incredible to me and brought me right into the Abbey of Gethsemani where I lived all during the reading of the book and long afterwards. I didn't want the book to end. I read it slowly savoring each holy entry and wished and prayed and longed to be a Catholic. In all the many spiritual books I read by Catholic authors and saints I would say that this particular journal set me afire the most and almost drove me crazy in the spiritual sense — with the deep, deep longing for my entrance into the Church. Thomas Merton's journal revealed the richness of the Catholic faith to me showing how each day was most important and filled with Jesus through the receiving of His Body and Blood in Holy Communion and visits before the Blessed Sacrament and through the celebration of the Feast Days that continually were with us. And above all he let me feel his great desire to be alone with Jesus more and more in precious solitude and told of his great love and devotion to Our Blessed Mother. I too, felt this love and devotion to Her when I prayed to Her faithfully as a Protestant for my miracle of entry into the Catholic church. I treasured the

Rosary I used. Merton was a very beautiful and powerful influence in my spiritual journey and rereading portions of his journal this second day of Retreat took away tears and fears and replaced them with joy and gratitude that I now had that miracle fulfilled that I had desired and craved all during the first reading of his journals years ago. I stopped and I prayed and somehow remembering all of this and the gift I had been given jostled me into a wonderful state and I hugged Rochester and just rejoiced within.

The phone ringing brought me Laurel when I answered — my second daughter and friend — and I shared with her about the book at Walden's and she asked advice about a problem troubling her in present weeks. We talked at length and I realized at the moment my hermitage was more like a Russian Poustinia where solitude is the beginning desire within a hut or cell with simple furnishings and only yourself before God — but it allows for interruptions for someone to come to your door and enter into your silence and be given help by you. Intrusion was expected in a Poustinia and never shunned. Help must always be given to the seeker even to the loss of your own aloneness. And so my daughter and I talked the concerns out and were better for it and closed in love — and I sent greetings to her Bob and the three boys.

There was no dinner because I had eaten breakfast and so the day and evening only held tea — several cups — and an herbal life drink for substitution of food. That was my agreement with myself. One solid meal per day. It was wonderful and I was glad to be adhering to it.

Chester was given his dinner and then he played as I wrote in my own journals — the smaller one meant only for this week apart — and in my regular one. This consumed a great portion of the evening, but writing fulfilled me and I could have gone on much longer than I actually did. More calls from home at intervals were very special — first June — my oldest daughter, wife of Rob, and mother of two sons and two daughters, thoughtful and kind as always, followed by Janna and Bob together on the same call to say goodnight.

My evening was still fresh however because I kept extremely late hours regularly at home for reading and writing — and my Retreat would be the same. I continued in this manner until 2:30 AM or so with Chester near me or on me curled up in sleep. I welcomed the early morning hours when others slept and the quiet of the night and darkness were present. It was a very spiritual portion of every twenty-four hours. I celebrated it then and really reveled in it. I began thinking more and more about my writing as I made the long entries in my journal. Praying again as I ended the day that I might write for Him — that it might be my vocation in life from this moment on and that the breakthrough I waited so long for might occur, I drifted off to sleep on the sofa under the same precautionary conditions of the previous night.

"The Nest," E. Wakefield, New Hampshire.

Part Eight

"I cannot! I cannot write this book about those disturbing relationships which involve such crucial problems, to name a few, as accepting rejection, understanding abandonment, and living with verbal or nonverbal abuse. I cannot show anyone my scars. I cannot deal with the problems of handling difficult people — Irregular People. I cannot!"
— Joyce Landorf

My wakeup call came again from Jenkintown, but this time from my son George whom I was so glad to hear — for it had been several days since we had spoken. Bob was on the line as well. And all before my alarm had gone off! Dressing and then caring for Chester I drove to Mass and the same five friends were there to begin our day with Jesus. After brief stops at the Post Office and store I again went to the Nest and found myself not so timid upon walking to the door but still very much in a state of unease while being seated. More people were present today and this was unnerving. I had brought a book along to read and to help keep them all a safe distance and I buried myself in ''The Power of Your Subconscious Mind'' while waiting. My waitress was the same young woman as the previous morning and she was friendly and kind and we exchanged small conversation in the course of my stay there. Her presence definitely helped me in this fear I was conquering. My breakfast was very small but I again had the muffin for my ''Muffins'' back home and enjoyed the coffee and left. I felt that He was making me stronger. While in the grocery store earlier I had taken a few moments to browse in the new video cassette section and there I came across a film that I believed had to have been put in my path by Jesus. I had

39

read some time ago and more than once — a book called "Irregular People" by Joyce Landorf and in this book another book
is spoken of as a perfect example of the existence of "Irregular
People." The second book was called "Summer of My German
Soldier" and I had yet to find it so I might read further on this
painful subject. But here before me was a movie by that very
name — and I just could not believe I could be that fortunate.
Joyce Landorf too — had first viewed the movie on television
and later read the book. The matter under discussion in "Irregular People" dealt with the severe problem that my friend at the
high school reunion had spoken of and was also a great part of
the new book I had bought on Monday at Walden's. The new
book, however, went much deeper on an extension of this original problem and actually covered much more in my life situation.

I rented the movie for later that evening and believed it would
be another asset for my Retreat — something I was meant to find
and view and to help me in this time alone and in future healing.

Some years before — perhaps three or four — my daughters
June and Laurel attended a visual seminar given by Joyce Landorf
— Christian author and speaker — on screen. It was presented
over a period of weeks at their Methodist Church in Jenkintown.
A new subject was presented, discussed and dealt with each
week. One day they came to me with a hardback book — and
it was my copy of "Irregular People". They had bought it for
me after attending the seminar on that subject. They had cried
through the session as had many others who were present —
because each was being touched by God and could see how the
Irregular Person in their lives had affected their overall Christian
walk. My girls realized in a new way as they listened, much that
I had experienced due to the situation I had lived with for many
years. They saw how the tentacles of this Irregular Person
reached out and touched many in the family, but basically it was
because the person first became the Irregular Person to ONE.
Through that one's emotional torment as the emotional and psychological blows were dealt day in and day out — the one
wounded affected other lives though not in a cruel sense — while

the tormentor affected the wounded one. Never had I heard the term before of "Irregular Person" nor had my daughters — but Joyce Landorf had one who caused her endless pain, and through her travels and teachings she learned that all over the United States others suffered from a person or persons like this — usually someone close to them and often a family member. It was a term that indicated that the irregular one was truly that — that what you would expect from one in a Christian walk — kindness, love, support, understanding, unselfishness, caring and more — simply was not there. The painful thing was that one just could not seem to accept this, that had an Irregular Person tormenting him. Always they hoped that next encounter would be peaceful and normal and good, charitable feelings would be there and when the encounter proved otherwise, then the one hurt went deeper into his wounds and depression. Often the Irregular Person seemed charming to others and this dark side was kept hidden from the outside world. Often they were spiritual leaders.

In my own life this had caused me defeat and despair. It brings confusion and one begins to doubt that he is even a Christian if one can feel such awful feelings within oneself after a meeting with his Irregular Person or through thoughts of him that keep passing through one's mind. I had sought prayer of healing for this frequently and each time would be stronger following the prayers, but then a blow or blows would be dealt and back I was in the pit again. Combined with the terrible offshoots of trouble in my personal life and that of my immediate family that this Irregular Person caused through the original problem, there were often days when alone after being emotionally struck down by this individual in our family, that I wanted to walk out of my home, get in the car and drive to where he was and physically strike out. Could this be a Christian's thoughts? On several occasions I had gotten as far as the car and driven, either driving aimlessly for a period and then returning home still in tears — or actually driving near that person's home and sitting some distance away feeling chained and helpless because I could not do what I planned.

This entire situation was another instrument God used in bringing me into the Catholic church despite all apparent obstacles, because my reactions to my Irregular Person after so many years of attempting to resolve it — were often so violent within and out of character to my true nature of timidity and shyness — that I felt maybe I truly was wicked and losing control and I sought confession within the Catholic church even while still a Protestant. Through this Sacrament and the accompanying counseling and prayers by a priest and friend — I found new direction and healing for many years. It was just in these last two years or so that new onslaughts were baffling me and dragging me down because they came in combination with other matters I was trying to set straight in my life and why I was here on Retreat. In the past my husband would tell me to draw a big zero on a paper and tack it above our phone. Then when talking to my Irregular Person — though at that time this term was not known — I was to expect just "that" from him — nothing! Zero! Anything in addition to that would be a surprise and small gift. I did it often by drawing the zero on the chalk board near by — but it rarely helped. There was "zero" in the normal ways a person should be but "not zero" in regard to the hurt they put forth. In reading the book given to me by my daughters it was a relief to see that I was not alone and that my feelings were not even abnormal in response. However, the book discovered at Walden's took it all a step further and encompassed the offshoots and extensions caused by the Irregular Person and how these in turn brought even more heartbreak and evil. Both books also gave beautiful help if the one with this problem was strong enough to adapt it — but the second book was an absolute for me to read for the first had not carried it quite far enough for the situation I had lived within. As I returned to the cottage and Chester I thanked God for allowing me to find this video cassette and for my more successful outing at breakfast in the homey little restaurant of which I was so fond. Onward now to important things — matters of the heart and soul and mind. Back to the woods and lake and the solitude so blessed. Onward! I couldn't wait.

Part Nine

"This is to tell you about a young man named Ernest Hemingway, who lives in Paris (an American), and writes for the TRANSATLANTIC REVIEW and has a brilliant future...I'd look him up right away. He's the real thing."
— F. Scott Fitzgerald to Maxwell Perkins — 1924

Writing was front and center in my heart as I returned to the cottage. Remembering my prayer of the night before I hoped that today would be the day I could write one sentence for Him aside from letters and the journal entries. Ernest Hemingway said: *"All you have to do is write one true sentence. Write the truest sentence that you know."* Ernest Hemingway's advice and writing disciplines meant a great deal to me. Since his coming into my life he has influenced my thinking in the area of the writing I longed to do. In fact the mere mention of his name makes me want to grab pad and pencil and sit down and write. I say pencil — I, who am so accustomed to using my favorite pen that my daughters even accuse me of doing commercials about it in my delight over it — because that is what Hemingway used. He wrote descriptive passages in his "Moveable Feast" about his actual writing practices — the what of writing, the where, the how and his love of writing. These passages drove me wild interiorly and I copied them all down in my Commonplace Book meant for quotations that touched my soul — the same book that held the many passages written by Thoreau and Merton and Dickinson and St. Francis deSales and other friends from all walks of life from the past and present. Hemingway wrote in "A Moveable Feast" — his autobiographical account of his early years in Paris as a writer and a very young man:

"The blue backed notebooks, the two pencils and the pencil sharpener (a pocket knife was too wasteful), the marble topped tables, the smell of early morning, sweeping out and mopping were all you needed. For luck you carried a horsechestnut and a rabbit's foot in your right pocket. The fur had been worn off the rabbit's foot long ago and the bones and the sinews were polished by wear. The claws scratched in the lining of your pocket and you knew your luck was there."

He actually made me feel as if I was there in that small cafe where he wrote throughout the day and I longed to find a cafe of my own — to be buried in some distant booth or far away table and write about life as it passed before me. And so loving Hemingway and his dedication to his craft caused me when reading him to even smell the pencils and know the feel of them in my hand, experience the opening of a notebook and realize the thrill of filling a page. I even bought a little pencil sharpener! I was crazed! I longed to write! When I'd read: *"It was a pleasant cafe", warm and clean and friendly, and I hung my old waterproof on the coat rack to dry and put my worn and weathered felt hat on the rack above the bench and ordered a cafe au laut. The waiter brought it and I took out a notebook from the pocket of the coat and a pencil and started to write. I was writing about up in Michigan and since it was a wild, cold, blowing day it was that sort of day in my story"* — (Moveable Feast) — I tasted the cafe au laut! I felt the warmth of that pleasant cafe and heard the winds blowing and felt the excitement of the fresh new day he was encountering that would be one of writing and filling the notebook with that wonderful story written with that wonderful pencil by that wonderful writer. I repeat myself even now in the telling of it all because I repeatedly read such passages, repeatedly longed to be there, repeatedly begged to be able to write and have such a life as this — dedicated to one's calling and dream. Mine was writing but I could not empty myself as he did. This retreat and this very day had to be the beginning of a new way for me — a writer's way.

As I read other authors I learned I was not the only one who felt the impact of Hemingway as a writer. He was quoted over and over again and each quotation I encountered I savored. Hemingway's willingness to help new or younger writers I admired — and also his reputation for generosity and loyalty to his friends. One well known friend of his — a film star for many years, Marlene Dietrich — has been quoted in one of Hemingway's biographies as saying very lovingly on his behalf — *"That's the wonderful thing about him — he kneels himself into his friends' problems. He is like a huge rock, off somewhere, a constant and steady thing, that certain someone whom everybody should have and nobody has."* Hemingway has said with regard to friendship — *"The way to learn whether a person is trustworthy is to trust him."* — Personally I value that truth. Applying it, however, has brought painful disappointment on a number of occasions.

I learned he was a convert to the Catholic faith as Merton and myself and I prayed for Hemingway's soul and Thoreau's each morning at Mass in gratitude for their inspiration to my soul and their devotion to writing. One writer showed me the minute particulars of the craft right down to the very way to sharpen a pencil, and the other showed me his discipline of keeping a daily journal and the seriousness and importance of such a task — of recording one's thoughts and observations. For Thoreau this became his life's work just as Hemingway's stories were his. And through it all I have come to give the pencil high regard as a writing tool for it helps to bring me close in spirit to these two men who also used and regarded it highly. Hemingway spoke of his pencils and included them in paragraphs that spoke of deeper and more meaningful matters and Thoreau — though a Harvard graduate — settled on making pencils and grinding graphite for his father rather than a vocation Harvard had prepared him for. This employment he allowed to take up only a small part of his time so that he might be free to walk about Concord with his pencil and paper recording his observations, and at night writing them out more completely and detailed in his journals. And so I gave the pencil new respect for in a June 4,

1839 entry in Thoreau's journal he wrote: — *"The words of some men are thrown forcibly against you and adhere like burs"* — and surely for me the words of Hemingway and Thoreau adhered to me in regard to the merest detail concerning their writing disciplines — right down to the very pencils they used. This quotation entered by Thoreau in his journal also brought to mind other significant writers — spiritual and otherwise and very especially Thomas Merton — who turned me around or made my soul stir just in the picking up of a well loved book.

I cannot remember how long ago or under what circumstance I had met Thoreau and come to know and love him and fill my journals with his journal entries and spend hours reading his words. I only know I was led to him by the Holy Spirit and met him when alone. But I very specifically remember Hemingway entering my life because it was far more recent. My introduction to Hemingway came through two trusted friends. It was precipitated by an inquiry after Mass by my poet friend, "Friar Francis", if I might know where to find the Elegy written by Thomas Merton to and for Hemingway following Hemingway's death. I knew immediately for I had seen it many times in my Merton Reader — a selection and compilation of Merton's choice writings. Because it had not been my time yet to discover Hemingway, the Elegy never was more than a title to me as I frequently read in the Reader. Oh, I had read the Elegy and liked it — but found no interest in searching more deeply into the life of Ernest Hemingway. My interest was in Thomas Merton — his writing, insights and poetry. However — once pointed toward Hemingway by my "Friar Francis", mutual lover of Merton — I read the Elegy in a new light and had deep interest in learning more about Hemingway. Somehow my education was lacking in this department for I had never read or studied Hemingway's life or works in high school as many students do and in Temple University I was in a professional vocation of Dental Hygiene — and Papa's writings were not included in the English courses in this field. Even as a young teenage girl I chose spiritual reading as my usual over fiction because I was very much a part of my Methodist

Church (although as a younger girl I read every Nancy Drew mystery book that was available) — and therefore I never had the pleasure of meeting Hemingway.

As I raised six children I continued to read spiritually — and also chose books in line with family life. There was so little time for reading in those years busy with children or for my love also of embroidery and machine sewing my first three daughters' clothes with outfits to match for their dolls. When I read then I chose only books that would matter and influence and help me — always non-fiction and ninety percent spiritual. I know now that there are beautiful truths and teachings in fiction also and that it is a difficult process to write a novel of worth — but that was not known to me until I was older. Hemingway was a figure I had heard spoken of but who never touched me personally. Obviously the timing was God's — for once I read the Elegy in dead seriousness and realized the admiration my spiritual friend Merton had for this man, I knew then I had to learn more about him and "meet him" soon.

Even before I could actively do anything about it myself — I believe Our Lord saw that I stumbled over two copies of "Papa" — a biography by A.E. Hotchner, Hemingway's best friend — at a flea market that same week and I bought both so one could be given to my "Friar" friend at church who had asked me about the Elegy in Hemingway's honor. Once I began this biography the next week as I drove to New Hampshire in September 1985 with my husband — I was Hemingway's friend forever.

As with words by and about Thoreau and Merton and other men I truly valued and read — I copied great passages from this biography by Hotchner into my Commonplace Book and thoroughly enjoyed every word I read in it while in New Hampshire. Since then it has been read twice more with other biographies that I hunted down and devoured about him — and then came the dessert — that of discovering "A Moveable Feast" — a "find" at a library book sale. This I've continued to read over beginning to end several times a year and refer to passages and chapters often in quicker rereadings from time to time. I keep an old hard-

back copy in Jenkintown on my Hemingway shelf and an old
hardback copy here in New Hampshire. A worn paperback of
same is kept in the small zippered tote bag with my journals and
Commonplace Book for easier reference or inspiration. Just one
passage read from it can cause me to write pages!

One day I will read all of his novels, but for this period in my
life I am content to know "the man". It is his life, his disciplines,
his love of his craft, his suggestions of titles of good literature
to read in order to write well, his love for others and his generous
heart, his humor, his sweet love for cats of which he had many
— and for his great autobiography of just one happy period in
his existence. "A Moveable Feast", that keeps me going, inspires
and drives my heart wild! Surely all these positive and loving
attributes outweigh the negative aspects in his life that someone
will occasionally try to point out to me. Haven't we all negative
aspects in our lives that we are not proud of? Don't we hope
and pray that the good we have attempted in life will be seen
in us and that we will not be judged forever by our mistakes?
Also his short stories are excellent reading to me for I can see
him writing them in that little cafe in Paris as a young man, pencil
in hand, rabbit's foot in back pocket, blue notebook open on the
marble top table as the waiter brings his cafe au laut. His framed
picture (a post card) as he was in Paris in 1926 sits on my writing
desk here in New Hampshire for inspiration — along with ones
of Our Lord and Blessed Mother. Papa is in their care now and
I believe all three are caring for me — each in a different way.

Today may I too be like that young man who had the call to
write. May this day — this week — be my time to pick up pencil
and open notebook and bring inspiration and fire to others
through the written word. May my writings no longer be confined to letters and journals. Just as Thomas Merton helped me
into the Catholic Church I believed with new conviction that he
gave me Hemingway and that Papa somehow would — through
the Communion of Saints — help me to write. "With God all
things are possible"* and in the dimension of the Spirit "more
things are wrought by prayer than this world dreams of."** It

*Scripture verse
**Tennyson

is written *"Some friendships are made by nature, some by contact, some by interest, and some by souls."* I thank Our Lord for my soul to soul friendships with my Magnifico Merton, my Heart-warming Hemingway and my Timeless Thoreau.

Taken on Retreat in New Hampshire as written about in "Higher Ground."

Part Ten

*"I never travel without my diary. One should always have
something sensational to read in the train."*
— Oscar Wilde

This new day of Retreat like a clean page in a book was about
to be written and some entries had already been made through
attendance of Mass and breakfast at the restaurant. Outwardly
it would seem uneventful to an observer had there been one —
but inwardly my spirit was being affected deeply by each little
occurrence. Being in solitude — like fasting — makes one's
"being" more sensitive to all about him and to all the stirrings
that are going on interiorly. So each thing done or experienced
as I went through the remainder of the day and into evening
seemed of more importance, and was received and reflected on
and responded to in a different dimension than had I been
amongst people and back home.

Therefore even finding my little Chester waiting was more
wonderful than usual and since he is always appreciated by me
— this reception for me was even sweeter. Writing in my journal
was a release for suddenly I was filled with words and they needed to be written. Page after page I filled effortlessly. There is nothing like writing it down straight from the heart — without pause
— just emptying oneself out onto the pages so that all goodness
and joy is captured forever and pain and sorrow flows out too.
The tears that often blur the eyes while the words are formed
and written are part of it all. Sometimes the tears are wordless
expressions that never make it onto the journal page except to
wet the words that do.

In the rereading of one's own journal at a time removed from the actual moments of the entries one can often become one's own therapist and counsellor and see deeply into woundedness and joy expressed there. Light can suddenly come into one's thinking and deepest revelations by the spirit can be seen, and as a result solutions can be found, healings begun and even correction and penance given to oneself over displeasure in attitudes or thoughts — or perhaps even actions. Journal keeping is such a complex discipline and practice that many books have been written on the subject and those persons that once discover and practice this can rarely be persuaded ever to give it up. For me it is like a running conversation with Jesus — a form of prayer perhaps and often, though certainly not always, ending in explicit prayer of gratitude, praise or special intentions and requests. That does not mean the actual entries are pious and spiritual. It is for me — as if I were merely speaking normally — no pretending. Just the real me — even at times a questioning, angry me. It is all for myself alone with Jesus listening in. On bad and upsetting days the writing seems heavy, untidy and mad and on regular or pleasant days the handwriting is neat and straight. The unlined pages in my regular journal allow the frustrated artist to be released also, for often when I allow more time I make flowered borders with colored pens or draw something that has come to mind with a small sketch. One drawing I particularly enjoyed doing and resulted with a pleasing likeness was that of my most used and loved Rosary given to me by my close friend on a significant evening, and cherished and used daily ever since. Not one brown wooden bead had escaped notice in the drawing of it and whenever I accidentally meet up with that page, it always brings happiness and memories of the receiving of the Rosary and the joyful events surrounding it.

When writers I admire describe their methods and tools and disciplines of their writing craft it is like a spiritual experience to me to read of this. It is the same then when I read the particulars of journal keeping and the fulfillment involved by journal keepers other than myself.

Many of these journal keepers are the writers I admire and read. A discovery I've made is that most writer's are devoted readers, and frequently journal keepers and letter writers as well. All of these addictions are mine and drive me spiritually wild and keep me going. Hemingway has a volume of letters I enjoy reading from often — wonderful and funny letters at times — which he admittedly loved writing and sending and bemoans the fact that letter writing seems to be a fading means of communication because people spend too much of their time before the television instead of keeping in touch in this wonderful way with their friends. His letters to friends were frequently filled with *"Come on down"* and *"Come on up"* and *"I miss you"*. Letters show the heart of a man or woman to the receiver but even more deeply is the heart exposed in a journal.

One journal keeper writes — *"I am going to ration myself on this dope of journalizing, make new rules. No writing here until after the novel-writing stint is over."* Like letter writing, journals can keep one from the main writing or activity one should be doing — and yet for Thoreau journal keeping was all! An author writes — *"I shouldn't write one word here this morning. Journalizing, like reading, should be the sweet which goes after the meat and potatoes, not before. But this morning I'm having the sweet first."* If *"To Sing is to Pray Twice"* — a quotation often seen on greeting cards and posters and attributed to St. Augustine — then to write or keep a journal is often said to "live twice". A writer I discovered only several weeks ago, Natalie Goldberg — but who is now like a close friend standing by as I write — states in her book "Writing Down the Bones" that *"Writers live twice. They go along with their regular life and are as fast as anyone in the grocery store, crossing the street, getting dressed for work in the morning. But there's another part of them that they have been training. The one that lives every thing a second time. That sits down and sees their life again and goes over it. Looks at the texture and details."* — This is so true for myself, for if I fail to write down a thought or experience or moment that I intended to keep permanently recorded, I am angry with myself. If it isn't entered quite promptly then a certain quality is lost when it finally is entered.

Emerson has stated in this regard: *"Look sharply after your thoughts. They come unlooked for, like a new bird seen on your trees, and if you turn to your usual task, disappear; and you shall never find that perception again, never, I say — but always years, ages, and I know not what events and worlds may be between you and its return."*

That is an overwhelming reflection and I can attest to its truth for too often beautiful thoughts and moments I intended to capture disappeared like a migrating bird and to this day have not returned to me. It is why I carry a small journal with me to help prevent this from happening, yet even this practice isn't foolproof.

It is worthwhile to "live twice" even if all we have retained in our journals does not bring happiness in the entering of it or in the rereading. It serves — no matter what emotion is involved — to aid us. This I believe, for if we were inspired to give our time to the writing of it, then I have found that the Lord often uses it at a later date for some special reason of His own in our life. We may not always discover why we were led to write it all down but that does not negate that what is deeply there for us if we also take the time to search it through.

Jessamyn West writes so beautifully also about the concept of "living twice". *"Sometimes I think I'm the luckiest woman in the world and tonight is one of those times. I like to write. I have pen, paper and a room of my own in which to do my writing. Writing is so difficult that I often feel that writers, having had their hell on earth, will escape all punishment thereafter. At other times, tonight for instance, I fear there will be no heaven for us. What joys can equal the writing of seven pages which I did today or this room and the pen and ink with which to relive the day? People who keep journals have life twice. I know there is a feeling that journal keepers are deficient in some way, book keepers of life rather than spenders. I used to think that if it were known that I, like Pepys and Evelyn, like Emerson and Thoreau, was a journal keeper it would increase my friends' regard for me. It doesn't. I suppose journal keeping is a kind of talking to one's self — and that seems queer to everyone. But dead journal keepers are my joy. If a writer of journals has life twice, the writer who read journals has it three times. To my mind, no other kind of writing gives the reader so much the feel of what another person has experienced."*

A journal is never a substitute for family or good friends nor is it to be a replacement for the love and emotional support others can give. But neither is the guidance and counsel of others a replacement for the self guidance a journal can give because insights that came to you through being in touch with your own inner being and wisdom may be far better and more valid than advice other persons supply. Also through prayer the Holy Spirit can enlighten and instruct.

Sitting down with your journal — that very simple act — is a symbol of a desire and readiness to enter another dimension and to be in communion with yourself. Unknowingly you may find self-healing and new visions and a recreating of self in the very act of picking up pen and writing. It is a mystery. There are no rules for writing in your journal and you can not do it wrongly and healing can come to you through words you might least expect.

With your own personal journal you do anything in it you wish. You can use any type of book, any pen or pencil, any language, and you can misspell or be correct — sloppy or neat, change your views or handwriting, the actual book you are using, your pen and your subjects. Anything goes! Everything goes! — because it is yours alone! You can draw in it, paste in photos or clippings — write unsent letters to friends or family members to see how you change as a person when writing to each individual. The possibilities are endless. You will find as you go along what suits you best and even that may change the more you become a steady journalist. You need change. You may keep one journal or several for reasons only you understand. These might be of different colors to signify what you choose the colors to signify — or they may vary in size. A journal is not a day by day diary as we often remember a diary from our childhood with limited lines and lock and key and meant for brief entries of weather or comments about boyfriends or proms or one's school work. A journal is so much more and used in complete freedom and meant for total expression, and many pages can be used at one writing and not merely one small lined page or space. You create your journal. It is conceived in your spirit and born as a living extension of yourself emotionally, psychologically and spiritually.

Katherine Mansfield — a favorite journal keeper of mine whose journal entries inspire me in relation to writing and love and who also wrote very fine short stories — writes as I frequently do — speaking to the Lord. Yet she does not always do this and I do not either. An entry in this prayer form from her journal reads: [Wednesday, December 1915] — *"Today I'm hardening my heart. I am walking all round my heart and building up the defenses. I do not mean to leave a loophole even for a tuft of violets to grow in. Give me a hard heart, O Lord! Lord, harden my heart!"*

I like Katherine Mansfield. I have come to know her through her journal. Sadly she died in her early thirties never to continue her beloved writing that she lived to do — yet years later other journal keepers like myself are inspired to go on and not to give up writing because of words long ago entered in her journal for her own help and reflection on her personal life and relationships, on her poor health and on her craft of writing. One entry will speak only of her striving to be better. *"May 31, 1919 Work. Shall I be able to express one day my love of work — my desire to be a better writer — my longing to take greater pains. And the passion I feel."*

The next entry may again be more reflective and spiritual such as this one of December 15, 1919. *"Honesty (why?) is the only thing one seems to prize beyond life, love, death, everything. It alone remaineth. O you who come after me, will you believe it? At the end truth is the only thing worth having; it's more thrilling than love, more joyful and more passionate. It simply cannot fail. All else fails. I, at any rate, give the remainder of my life to it and it alone."*

Though she writes this as if for future generations, her journal was most private to herself alone. It was her husband, after her death — who published her cherished journals.

And so I close my journal now after writing and having spent a long period absorbed in thought — longer than I realized for much time had passed. It was not time wasted, however, for I knew I was with Him and I felt refreshed and calmer. Now I must move on to other things and return to my journal later. It would remain there waiting and for that I was thankful. Like a faithful friend it was always there accepting me just as I was — and allowing me to pour myself out. And so was my precious little Rochester with his unconditional love. As I hugged him to me I couldn't stop smiling thinking about a little poem that had instantly come to mind when I recalled Katherine Mansfield's husband and his publishing of her private journals. It was humorous advice given by a woman who taught the subject of journal keeping — an instruction to inscribe in the flyleaf of one's private journal if worried about its destination if one should become sick or die;

Now I lay me down to sleep
I pray the Lord my soul to keep
If I should die before I wake
Throw my journal in the lake!

Now that inscription I should appropriate — with all of Lake Balch outside my door!

Part Eleven

*"It's so frustrating, because you can't reason with them,
can't depend on them, and can't expect any real support
from them — Irregular People don't merely "bug" us —
they wound, stab, pull out chunks of our heart, and the
poison darts hit deeper as the relationship continues."*
— from "Irregular People"

Quickly straightening up the slight disorder I had created in
the living room I made a cup of tea and sat down to do more
reading. I had just gotten settled and Rochester had circled about
several times to find the most comfortable place on my lap when
the phone rang. It was my daughter Jessica calling from work
just to greet me and make sure that I was fine. We exchanged
some news and had some fun and she shared a sweet happening
about her beloved dog, Katie — when suddenly at the close of
the conversation she mentioned the Irregular Person in my life,
because the person had entered her life briefly since I had been
gone. We said our goodbyes and I was so pleased she had called
— but now the closing mention of the Irregular Person stuck with
me and I was angry at myself for letting the mention of the person
affect me. I was churning inside also that this person had in-
truded into my day and into my Retreat so directly — not just
through my thoughts that I had brought along with me because
I could not rid myself of them — but that I had to hear actual
present news of the person. I did not want to know anything
about this. My Retreat was to help me get this person out of my
inner being and mind so I could get peace and relief, yet at the
same time reach the point of acceptance that they would never
go! Why did I have to hear the person's name audibly spoken

into my sacred peace of Retreat? Now I was restless and discontent and felt almost helpless. How far did I have to go to escape this person and the mention of the name and the effects upon me? Wasn't 400 miles away far enough? If I couldn't escape at this distance then I felt I needed help more than ever. It was disturbing I could feel such emotion and have tears and restlessness and have even a small portion of these precious hours in solitude spoiled just because this person had acted in their usual irregular way that should be expected and I was informed of it so promptly by phone into my little cottage so very, very far away. Yet my daughter did not do this with intention to hurt me but with the desire to receive my advice. Inside myself I was going berserk and knowing from past experience it could become worse if I allowed it. I sat down immediately again with Rochester and read great portions of the book that I had been led to at Walden's. In the reading of this book I was reading positive passages and actual happenings that seemed almost lifted out of my life as the examples written about in this new book, and there was hope given that there could be a possible solution though not in every case. But at least to read it made me feel like a normal human being and that I hadn't been confused and mentally disturbed all these years — that this was a very real and threatening situation and I was not the one responsible. To at least know that now and to realize that all the times in years past when I doubted myself so frequently because of the dreadful confusion this situation caused in my heart and soul that I was having a normal reaction to this ongoing problem was a step into healing. I was meant to feel confused — meant to feel disturbed and often told I was the one totally at fault for the problems. And so this new book gave affirmation as never before and was as if Jesus himself had stepped in to explain everything to me. I felt His presence and more tears came for I knew most certainly He had caused this book to be in my path and was using this author's words to speak to my soul.

Since then I have also read directly the words from the book "Summer of My German Soldier" by Betty Greene — the words that caused Joyce Landorf to title her book "Irregular People" and to write on this subject that had affected her own life so terribly. Her book and the one found at Walden's were a prescription for sanity and realization and true illumination for me on the matter that had been a darkness in my life for many years and that had caused ongoing ripples of more pain and humiliation. The words I read directly from "The Summer of My German Soldier" sometime after my Retreat are spoken by Ruth — a black housekeeper. She is speaking to Patty Bergen about her parents who are always mean and irritable to Patty and who have never given her acceptance or approval. The mother seemed to have no opinion in her life and any affection she shows is for Patty's younger sister, Sharon. But the father is seen in another way — filled with conflicting emotions and responses — sometimes freezing cold — sometimes hot — often lukewarm and occasionally even loving. Sometimes he is there for Patty in a supportive and fatherly way — almost too nice! At other times he is uncaring and totally insensitive. And occasionally he would beat her with his belt. The terrible confrontation by her father that Patty had just gone from to the safety of Ruth's arms is described by Joyce Landorf as a witnessing of one human being raping another human being's soul. Patty was utterly destroyed and shattered. Ruth had defended Patty repeatedly and therefore Patty's father had fired Ruth sometime before. But Patty runs from this horrendous encounter into Ruth's kitchen and into her open arms and Ruth comforts her and strokes her hair and speaks these very profound but simple words to Patty about parents she could never please no matter how hard she tried — not now or ever.

—*"but your folks ain't nevah gonna feel nothing good regarding you. And they ain't the number one best quality folks neither. They shore ain't. When I goes shoppin' and I sees the label stamped "Irregular" or "Seconds", then I know I won't have to pay so much for it. But you've got yourself some irregular seconds folks, and you've been paying more'n top dollar for them. So just don't go a-wishing for what ain't nevah going to be."*

And Patty replied: *"But I always thought it was me. Because I was bad." "You ain't bad"! — came Ruth's firm answer "And I'm telling you, Miss Patty Bergen, we is the only ones that matter — cause we ain't irregular. Now you stand up straight. You is a whole person — a creature of God and a thing that matters in this world. Straighten up, girl. You got person-pride from this day on. And I don't never wanta see you slopin' your shoulders or your soul again. Not never!"*

Such wisdom from the loving Ruth who truly loved and cared for Patty and who tried to be her buffer in the irregular household that Patty inhabited and her parents cruelly ruled. The new book from Walden's I was reading and "Irregular People" and the passage from "Summer of My German Soldier" all rolled into one became "My Ruth" — my help and consolation — and gave me answers and explanations I had sought for years. How Jesus has used books in my spiritual journey to show me His truth and direct me! Books have been my comfort and guidance and stepping stones to a deeper spiritual life in Jesus, to the Catholic church and to fragments of healing here and there and for the beginning hopefully — of the alleviation or subduing of this situation in my life and for the gradual removal of fears.

The afternoon passed and He quieted my inner turmoil through the reading and prayer — and a walk outside by the lake. The breezes washed over me and I felt renewed and with a right spirit to go indoors and continue my Retreat on a higher plane and willing to be helped and healed.

Though I had eaten breakfast and had planned to be strict with myself I succumbed to eating two brown rice cakes with my tea and fed Chester his favorite food and vitamins to prepare us for our evening together.

As I sipped a new cup of tea with Chester close beside me on the sofa — we watched "Summer of My German Soldier" using the video cassette I had rented. It was beautifully done — a tender but tragic story one can never forget — though I vehemently shared Joyce Landorf's fury at the overbearing father. Joyce had actually yelled out at the father on television — so stricken was she by his behavior. When Ruth spoke her famous words to Patty

I felt Ruth's arms about me also. Chester didn't mind that I cried all through the movie. He frequently came to stand on the front of me with his sweet little furry face about an inch from mine to examine me more closely and get wet with my tears when he'd bump his little head against me — his way of kissing and wanting kisses in return on the front of his little forehead. He knew I was upset. After quietly recovering and thinking about it for some time — I replayed portions of it to view again and to absorb the scenes and words that most ''struck home''.

How alike was my Irregular Person in so many ways with Patty's parents — particularly with her father. How often had this Irregular Person of mine bestowed rejection or attempted to force their will upon me — or upon others within my immediate family. It went back years and continued into the present. In personal dealings the irregular one showed favoritism, showering love and concern in one area and apparent apathy in the other — and the favoritism was flaunted! This certainly is a form of deliberate cruelty — because it was continuously repeated. It also becomes real abuse when hard worked for success is ignored in one person while continued tribute is being paid to another. Respect is expected by the Irregular Person from all — and despite the pain that this one gives — all give respect in return for we all are loving Christian people. There is day in and day out trauma of dealing with such an individual and most defeating and despairing is the confusion of mind and spirit that comes from all association with this person. It becomes torment to envision the Irregular one's face and to actually have to be in their company and to see the mask they wear for others.

Examples of this cruelty filled my mind as I paraded event after sad event with my Irregular Person through my thoughts — and keen resentment rose in me like a nauseating sickness. How could I solve this? What were the steps I must take to purge my heart and mind of this presence which seemed so much with me — beating down my good intentions and in fact my entire personality into a mere shadow of the person I envisioned for myself. The answer seemed clear — it was the same answer to all of life's questions — Jesus!

"O dear Jesus — how I need your help. Thank you for showing me I have not been insane in the feeling that arose within my heart and mind and in my responses. Thank you for showing me through this film and this book you led me to on Monday — that I am not alone in the world concerning all of this — that others have been suffering under this same torment. Thank you for what you will do to heal me once and for all — and to give me acceptance of my Irregular Person. I trust in you anew on my spiritual Retreat."

I closed with a special prayer for our friend at the high school reunion and his Irregular Person who caused him deep anguish and pain.

Part Twelve

A faithful friend is the medicine of life
— Ecclesiasticus

A faithful friend is an image of God
— French Proverb

As I settled down once again on the sofa for sleep I heard noises outside the kitchen window — a crackling of twigs as a footstep would create. From experience I knew there were many animals in the woods that came right up onto our porch in the dark — but now I could only believe it was a human intruder. I could summon no courage to investigate. Fear took hold and once more I turned the television on very softly though the screen was covered with lines. I allowed a small lamp to remain on. The low indiscernible voices from the television blotted out any further outside noise and the lamp gave a comforting glow. Chester cuddled with me on the sofa and I held Crucifix and Rosary — as well as his dear little purring body beside me. On the small table next to the end of the sofa where I sat and also slept — were two religious pictures that I kept near me at home and also carried to New Hampshire each trip I made. One was a gloriously colored icon of Our Mother of Good Counsel — about 5 x 7 inches — all wooden and crafted magnificently — and it caused devotion to Our Lady with just the merest glance. It had been given to me years ago by my close friend shortly after I was received into the Catholic Church. Its home was in my prayer room on what I called my altar table — a table holding my dearest religious statues, pictures and treasures and before which I frequently knelt in prayer. Now my icon was again in New Hampshire with me breathing love and protection.

65

The other picture was also colorful and similar in size — but it held an image of Our Lord under the title of Señor de Los Milagras and was framed in wide ornate silver. It was a precious gift from my "otra familia" — "mi espiritual familia" — the Rodriquez's in Lima, Peru and on the wooden back of the image each family member I love had signed their name for me. It was an irreplaceable keepsake from loved ones who loved me and it had been given in deepest love and caring and carried safely from Peru to Jenkintown by one whose signature appeared on it. It was a symbol to me and to them that there is "no distancia en el corazon de Jesus" though thousands of physical miles separated us on earth. Since the time this picture had been given to me as finest "regalo" — the mother of this family had died just several months previous to this day — making the "gift" all the more pricelsss. Magdalena was my friend and sister in Christ and she had been terminally ill with cancer. While in the United States with her daughter Martha (my spiritual daughter) and having undergone tests in a Philadelphia main line hospital and learning this news as a result of tests — we became even more closely bonded as I undertook the love task of cooking macrobiotic meals for her for a period of five months in the hopes that a miracle would be given by Jesus using this special Japanese diet of nourishing food to remove the cancer and restore health. Our days together in her daughter's small apartment were joyful despite her pain and illness. Though she could speak no English and I knew little Spanish — we spoke heart to heart with our eyes and our hands and our laughter — and in pointing to pictures. We wrote down prayers for each other in our own languages so we could say them when apart and have the feeling of closeness as she attempted hers in English and I whispered mine in Spanish. I still have the book in which she entered her written Spanish prayers for me and I use it and ask her intercession now in Heaven. Her letters and gifts and photos of us taken together will always be kept and treasured and regrets enter my heart often that I never went to her and allowed her and her family to show me their Peru while she lived. Soon it was necessary for us to part after our weeks and months spent so closely together and she returned to Lima where another was taught to cook her special meals for her by her daughter who had accompanied her home. Martha had observed as I cooked and then helped me frequently in the cooking, and therefore could share the diet with a new cook before returning to the United States. All, except Martha, who signed my picture, Pedro, Charo and Armando — remained in Lima with my sick friend — though all had visited the United States several times. Jesus had given us this special bond from the first moment we had all met in Kennedy Airport upon their first arrival from Peru.

Our original discovery of each other had obviously been arranged by Jesus when He led my daughter June to take into her home my spiritual daughter Martha. She had come to the United States to study for her Masters Degree and through a chain of events she began to live with June and husband Rob and their children. When Martha and I were drawn together due to our Catholic faith she soon began to call me "Mom". I was her American Mom and her family was so grateful to Rob and June and to myself — and to my husband and all of our family. Now — though I will never ever replace my "sister and friend", Magdalena, — I do have an even greater responsibility to Martha — Magdalena's daughter and mine — for in Magdalena's illness and our times together alone she frequently gave her daughters to me. Her other two daughters remain in Peru while Martha lives in California with her husband. We are kept closely in touch by frequent weekly phone calls and letters and we thoroughly miss our Magdalena. Pedro — Magdalena's husband and my "bueno amigo" and I correspond and call long distance and pray. "Señor de Los Milagros" means Lord of the Miracles and in Peru He is always honored and a church bears His name and image on the church's inner wall. There is special devotion to Him all the month of October and Peruvians who are deeply pious and disciplined wear purple habits all of that month. Magdalena was always adorned in purple habit during October for her Señor — and in the privacy of her home wore it at other times also.

Those who cannot wear the robe frequently wear scapulars. His image is carried in great processions through the streets of Lima in this month and the special feast day is October 18th. I, too, have a scapular and feel honored that I do.

Though Magdalena suddenly died of a heart attack June 27, 1986 — she would tell you that never did her Señor ever fail her. Each time I look at this framed image or see any of my other religious objects from Peru that they continuously gave to me — I know dear Magdalena is with Him and her joy is full. And her life on this earth as I knew it influenced me for good and I was given the gift of "mi otra familia para siempre" by this precious Señor de Los Milagros and with Señor's help disciplined myself to learn enough Spanish that I could write my letters to them in their language, thus creating a deeper communication while apart. Gracias! Gracias! Gracias mi Señor.

And so with these memories in great loving detail filling my mind as I waited for sleep — I felt peaceful once more — and what possibly lay beyond my kitchen window never penetrated these thoughts or frightened me again. Señor was with me — and Our Blessed Mother also. I did not need these pictures to know this truth — but to kiss them each goodnight gave an inner strength their visibility and touchability provided.

Part Thirteen

*"By this shall all men know that ye are my disciples, if
ye have love one to another."*
— John 13:35 (King James Version)

Again my wake up call came from Bob before my alarm went
off. I had been awake until after 3 AM the night before but I was
always up early in the mornings despite my frequent later hours
both here and in Pennsylvania. Though there would be no Mass
today or tomorrow I still did not want to waste any time in sleep.
The week was passing too quickly and I was desperately trying
to slow it down by adding as much awake time as possible.

I would miss Mass terribly for I always began my mornings
with Our Lord and in receiving His precious Body and Blood.
But the priest here in Sanbornville had the responsibility for two
parish churches — the other church some distance away — and
often when problems or illness arose Mass could not be scheduled. I understood and would make frequent spiritual commu-
nions throughout today and tomorrow in place of actually
receiving Him in the Eucharist.

I hugged and played with Rochester then fed him breakfast
in his little white porcelain bowl with a little kitten's head and
feet at the front. I dressed and left Rochester enjoying breakfast
as I drove to the Nest for mine — and for continued self therapy
in conquering my restaurant inhibitions and fears.

More faces turned my way today as I entered and I felt embarrassed and awkward longing to turn back. But I didn't — and
the act alone of putting one foot before the other and heading
for obscurity in a corner made me somewhat surprised and proud

of myself. I slipped again into the red cushioned booth, laid my book on the table, pretended to check something in my pocket-book and then at last had the nerve to look up and glance about. A smile came from here and there which I returned and I chastened myself within for having been so bound up over a normal procedure like entering a restaurant and eating some food. Perhaps it even tied in with the word "food" — for food controlled me in that I had a fear of it. Perhaps it was the food and eating alone and admitting I was eating alone — that was the demon — or the basis certainly of the overall restaurant fear. I could only continue my prayers and believe that this Retreat would in some way carry me over this obstacle permanently leaving me free no matter what the cause.

My favorite waitress came to my table and I wanted again to tell her how she had helped and supported me this week without her having known. I wanted to tell her how her friendliness had strengthened my weakness and how her smiles and conversation made me forget my fears. Jesus had sent her to me each morning, I knew that.

As we talked about the weather while ordering my coffee she asked suddenly why I had been coming in each morning and why I was alone. She said it was very nice to see me each morning but she had seen me other times and other seasons with my husband and family and she was concerned that I was now without them. It had taken her several days to ask. I wondered if she would understand that I had come away to be alone. As I began to explain my aloneness and my Retreat and without going into great detail spoke of the purpose of such a week — she looked around to see if she was needed and assuring herself that she was not apparently — she slipped into the booth opposite me to listen. She was very interested and I could tell in her eyes she understood and asked several questions to learn more. She was thoughtful and quiet and then remarked that I must be most sincere about it all to come such a distance and to stay in the woods.

She sat for a moment in silence just looking at me and I at her — when suddenly she spoke again telling me that she admired the medals that I wore and had noticed them each time I was in. I confided their meaning to her and that I never removed them and she confided then to me that she was not Catholic but that her grandmother is and she loved her grandmother very much.

Again we fell silent and she glanced about the room making certain all was well. Few remained and all were content talking and eating in this very special little dining room with paneled walls and fluffy curtains and built in friendliness. It was a place one liked to remain to linger leisurely over coffee and converse with companions — so no one would demand her services, for this was country where there was courtesy and sociability and a warmness in spirit even among strangers — and always between guests and waitress.

She told me then with concern in her eyes and voice that she would not be seeing me tomorrow morning because her little nephew was very sick and was going into the hospital for tests and she wanted to be at the hospital with her family. She pulled out a picture from her pocket so that I might see the little boy and we shared this special moment together. I told her I would miss her and that I would pray for her nephew. Somehow she could not form that request but I felt it in her manner and saw it in her face and eyes that she was wordlessly asking for prayer.

After our goodbyes I found an old blank envelope in my pocketbook and wrote a few brief sentences of encouragement to her and that I would be praying. And I thanked her for her kindnesses — then I left it with her tip by my coffee cup.

God works in mysterious ways His wonders to perform — for in these mornings in this restaurant He brought together two women — very subtly and gently — to minister to each other in their concerns and fears. I had been looking for her after our first encounter as my anchor and friend in my self imposed therapy — and she had been observing in my wearing of religious medals and in my aloneness perhaps as one to confide in. We were there for each other and He had arranged it all. Praise be to God.

Part Fourteen

"Love all God's Creation, the whole and every grain of sand in it. Love every leaf, every ray of God's light. Love the animals, love the plants, love everything. If you love everything you will perceive the divine mystery in things. Once you perceive it, you will begin to comprehend it better every day. And you will come at last to love the whole world with an all-embracing love."

— Dostoyevsky

Following this encounter I briefly stopped in the local store for a small frozen dinner for myself and to look again at the video cassettes. I returned "Summer of My German Soldier" and glanced quickly over the empty boxes on the rack and almost immediately saw an autobiography that I felt I might like to view — an autobiography of a black woman Maya Angelou and the movie was made from her book "I Know Why the Caged Bird Sings". Since I kept very long hours into the early AM of the mornings and slept only 4 to 4½ hours — watching this auto-biography as I ate my small dinner would be a relaxing break from the seriousness of my Retreat goals and also informative. I left the store with a Lean Cuisine and the video cassette. If at dinner I wasn't inclined to watch then I would not — but I had rented it in case I might like such a change.

Chester welcomed me and we played. I tossed his favorite toy upon the kitchen floor — the round plastic circlet that is removed when a milk bottle cap is opened — and he chased it and held it in his paws and threw it upwards. These various colored circlets were his delight especially when I joined in — but he often spon-taneously pounced on one and made his own fun. Changing into older clothes and gathering up my books and Breviary, camera, and legal pad, pen and journal — I put them in my large canvas bag and went outdoors. It was an incredibly beautiful day — warm and sunny as if in summer — and my Retreat could take place outside just as well as inside. When here in summer I did spend most of my time outdoors doing anything and everything — just because it was such a blessing to be always near the sky, and water, and trees and be surrounded by scenery that made one feel grateful to be alive. Before leaving the cottage I pulled open the large front sliding doors so that Chester could also feel the sun and breezes yet still be protected by the large screens. His favorite spot for napping in summer was behind the sofa and next to the screen that separated the living room and the front porch. It was summer again for us this day.

Selecting a folding chaise lounge from the storage shed I dragged it down to the water's edge some 60 feet from the front of the cottage. I called reassurance to Chester and he was comforted that I was remaining right within his vision. Once in the chair I made my spiritual Communion and read my scripture and prayed and thanked God I could be doing all of this today in solitude surrounded by His great outdoors. The line from a poem by Browning came to mind — *"God's in His heaven — all's right with the world."* I suddenly saw that only when we let Him be loving Master of our own personal world can we know the peace and security that this line indicates. And if each human being that He created made Him Master — all these personal worlds in which He lovingly reigned would meld into one world of self-less love and harmony and joy and then and only then — could that line from poetry fulfill its deepest meaning. Pondering this I entered that place where one meets Jesus in wordless prayer and praise and presence and remained with Him for a period that knew no time. Only until He gently released me did I again actively begin my reading and searching — both through thought and journal writing. For me I had to see what I was thinking and sorting out and so I wrote and wrote from my heart. Oh that helped, for writing leads to healing and wholeness — and soon I found some resolutions were forming that I could hope to follow when I was forced to leave this precious solitude. There had to be guide lines for me given by Him and in this journal writing some had surfaced. I could not return to normal life in Pennsylvania as I had come from it — otherwise my Retreat had been in vain. Would I — by the last day or even this day — be aware of new strengths within myself, or changes — or missing fears? In this hope I went through my day out in the open under the heavens before Him.

I broke these thoughts momentarily to kick off my sandals and to roll up my jeans and wade in the water as I did in summer, with the idea to collect rocks. Rocks have been important to me since I was a child and while I had no collection of worth — I did have them here and there on bookcases, window sills, desk etc. Only I knew the significance of each one for each had been brought back either from New Hampshire or other states when on vacation — each representing a moment or thought or event of deep meaning to me personally. Most of them signified happiness of some sort — but one reminded me of an extremely sad and humiliating event and a sorrowful year to follow for it had a black band entirely circling the rock as if the rock were in mourning. It indeed was, for it was representing betrayals that had bound me in sadness and depression so that I couldn't be free — just as the lighter colored portion of this rock appeared bound in the black area that encircled it. But the rock also gave hope for in His strength and with the intercession of St. Joseph and the help of a fine priest counsellor from my parish I had broken out of that blackness. And my rock next to it on my shelf — all brilliant and sparkling with highlights of silica made me remember how I again came into the light. And knowing and remembering this gave me determination and new trust that He was continuing His work in me to make me new and whole and that this Retreat would indeed make a difference.

And so I began to collect rocks from beneath the lake and see if they qualified to bring in some way the meaning of this week to another — then I sat them along the grass above the water's

edge to dry — side by side in a line. Each one would be given
— personally chosen — to each of my friends from daily Mass
back home — my wonderful "Muffins". The rocks would represent the solitude of the woods and the lake, His utter strength
and also their source — for they were granite rocks in many
shapes and colors from New Hampshire — the granite state.

Happy and child-like with my completed collection and actually
knowing already who the new owners of several would be —
I went back to just "being". Changing my chair's position from
beach area to dock — I decided to just "be" in the warmth of
the sun without benefit of the tall trees I had been shaded by
earlier. Sun, pouring down makes one feel enveloped by Jesus
and with closed eyes one could in imaginative prayer and creative
visualization actually believe one was within the loving fiery
Sacred Heart of Jesus. And in the coolness under trees with
breezes strong — sometimes forceful from over the lapping water
— one has just a hint of the strength of the Holy One back of
those breezes that wash over one's being. In His creations He
lets us truly experience aspects of His divine nature if we are
open. Silence and solitude are just two of the gifts He provides
in order to go more deeply into His order.

"Being time" is essential in my life and can be time beneath
the trees or time wrapped in the sun — for it brings me closer
to Him and makes golden moments out of ordinary ones. It is
not wasted time but time spent well, for invisibly our soul is
touched and we are better for it. I am never bored at any moment
in my life because "in being" one can be transported to a higher
plane even in the midst of a crowd or while forced into a waiting
situation — and in "being" our minds and hearts are changed
and lifted. Ideas come, appreciation of others and creativity is
given opportunity to spark and come alive. If we give ourselves
over freely to frequent times of "being" and prayer — we will
never have boredom. Our lives are fed and nurtured by these
tiny sacred moments — small Retreats into His heart — and all
else that we are and do is affected.

Thoreau wrote:

"Sometimes I sat in my sunny doorway from sunrise until noon, rapt in a revery, amidst the pines and hickories and sumacs, in undisturbed solitude and stillness, while the birds sang around or glided noiseless through the house, until by the sun falling in at my west window, or the noise of some traveller's wagon on the distant highway, I was reminded of the pass of time. I grow in those seasons like corn in the night, and they were far better than any work of the hands would have been. They were not times subtracted from my life, but so much over and above my usual allowances. I realized what the Orientals mean by contemplation and the forsaking of work."

The revery of which Thoreau speaks just "happens" to us. It happens to me. In prayer chair by the lake very especially, or in prayer room in Pennsylvania, hours can pass. On one occasion such as this when "rapt in a revery" so described, a small sea plane actually landed on our lake a short distance from our shore line while I was in my prayer chair and within several minutes took off again. Not one moment of this unusual happening had I been aware of. I learned of it later from my family who had watched from the cottage and thought I was observing it too.

And so after time such as this in the sun — I turned to capturing the changing colors of the foliage along the water's edge with my camera. The gold and orange and red of the leaves became more brilliant in the slowly setting sun of late afternoon and early evening.

I returned to the cottage to capture also the inner beauty of my "Retreat taken outdoors"—by writing my heart thoughts in my journal. E.M. Forster has written *"How do I know what I think until I see what I say"*—and I say—"Amen". I reread a passage I had entered in my new journal meant for this week alone—a wonderful passage that made me overjoyed to be here in the woods each time I reread it—a passage entered to lift my soul, *"I have always noticed that people who keep company with the natural world, who live with mountains, plains, lakes, with the sun and the wind, the moon and the stars, are peaceful, joyous men and women, and they are nourished in their soul by a spirit that can flow only from God".* — John Muir — This — was Higher Ground!

Taken on Retreat. Scene along our shoreline, Lake Balch.

Part Fifteen

"I sit and listen for your voice, O Lord,
And the silence of the trees is what I hear.
I look for your reflection in the lake
And I see white clouds mirrored there.
And I reach out for you and feel the air,
And I remember you are Spirit
And my own spirit breathes you in"
— Fr. Murray Bodo, OFM
(from his journal)

I learned it was 4 PM upon my return and sat writing with the front sliding doors open and sun streaming in until 6:05 PM. The air and the sun felt so wonderful I decided to wander outside once again to take more pictures and sit in my prayer chair. Chester was sleeping beside me and I quietly left him so he wouldn't realize my absence. Pictures taken this time of the day of the shoreline and lake had more intense color and clarity, and reflections of the trees and clouds in the water were so sharp and defined that one could not tell reality from reflection if the photo were turned upside down. I never tired of taking pictures of all this splendor and most especially of the sunsets upon the lake. In my photo collection were the golden and pink sunsets — usually of summer — and the deep burning orange that seemed most brilliant in the starkness of winter when the ground was snow covered, the water frozen and the trees bare. One has to experience the sunsets. Words cannot do them justice. My photographs come closest to revealing their true wonder and beauty.

The photography session finished — with my big canvas bag I climbed up onto the platform by the water that holds my prayer chair, and settled into the chair to think and pray and enjoy the breezes. This truly was a Holy place to me. I thought about how blessed I was to have such an unusual place for prayer and began to reflect back on how long I had been privileged to call this place my own and how it came to be.

I remembered the summer of 1976 my family and I had gone to buy redwood furniture for our cottage. It was an outdoor sale at a fine furniture store about eighteen miles from here. As I strolled around in the crowd alone, suddenly there it was! It was not something that just anyone would want — or at least not for the reason that I wanted it. I thought it most magnificent and also most extraordinary that it should be put in my path. I touched it and walked around it and mentally placed it in position and then placed myself upon it.

I felt the wind, the sun, the night air and heard the birds and crickets — and I knew I was standing before a spiritual treasure. I needed it more than food or clothing! If I couldn't have it then I wished I had never seen it. A salesman was walking among the customers and I asked him the price. He had appeared just as I abruptly came free of the reverie in which I had allowed myself to slip after encountering this monumental "find". "Just $10.00", he had said — "It's one of a kind". Now as I recalled this scene — my original joy came over me again. There was my beautiful chair! Oh, it was no ordinary chair! Oh no indeed!

It was a lifeguard chair — tall and wooden! It had three steps to climb before reaching the seat and there were wooden arms to hold one in and make one feel secure and comfortable. The back and seat were closely arranged wooden slats and the entire chair was painted gray. I never regretted for a moment the purchase of what might be an outlandish white elephant to others. It has served me well for six long years. It had never failed to live up to the expectations I had placed upon it.

It had not remained gray. My husband who wielded his paint brush frequently — had painted everything green on the premises to match the cottage. But the fresh coat of paint only made it appear more exceptional — and so green it remained.

I had placed it by the water's edge under three extremely tall

Prayer Chair overlooking Lake Balch.

pines and surrounded by some lower trees and shrubs. And there it settled in and took root for almost the remainder of its life.

I, too, almost took root then, for it was my favorite spot to be. It was my place of solitude; my hermitage, my poustinia, my cell — my prayer chair! It was in this chair I met the morning and renewed my wonder of the blue lake and view before me. It was in this chair that I prayed many times throughout the day. It was to this site I came when troubled or overjoyed. It was in this chair perched high above the water that I wrote my letters and journals and read my books and took endless pictures — that I might always have these perfect moments in which the lake was exceptionally blue or the sunset particularly orange. It was from this height I most enjoyed my children as they in turn enjoyed their beautiful surroundings.

And it was in this prayer chair I remained alone in the dark for hours while the prevailing breezes from the lake came upon me and the night noises of the woods filled my silence and my communion with God. It was from this perch I saw the full moon reflecting upon the water and experienced perfect peace.

It was in this chair I had felt the night wind wash over me after travelling 400 miles from Pennsylvania following my Father's death. Only there and then had the tears finally been released. I had come to this spot for healing of soul and spirit.

The chair was respected in my family's eyes and all knew it could only be used by individual family members for quiet times; pondering, reading and enjoying the wonders of the scenes about them. Friends miles away longed to hear about my hours in my prayer chair and those spiritually oriented as myself — lovingly envisioned such a hallowed place of aloneness. It was all I hoped it would be and far more wonderful.

But despite all of the joys of this chair and the treasure it had been — a sadness was there. The chair had been second hand when I purchased it and though it had been repaired now and again the minute a flaw appeared — I learned one day that the wood was rotten within and now beyond fixing. It was a danger to climb upon and the precious chair of prayer had come to its time of retirement.

I wouldn't part with it until a replacement could be made and disregarding warnings I continued to many times daily climb in and out of the high place. I could never believe my chair would harm me. And from the aged and crippled chair I prayed that soon a new one would be found so that I might not continue to burden the present one. Oh how I would miss this precious friend who held me and lifted me closer to God. I captured its worn loveliness with my camera so that I might have it with me in picture form always.

Before the chair could break down completely and collapse upon the ground or cause injury — my prayers were answered for a new one. So earnestly did I pray and so involved was I in protecting my blessed friend in its old age — I did not take full notice of some carpentry that was being performed near by. Soon, very gently my husband moved the high chair just slightly to one side, and down below in the very spot on which it had stood all these many years — he began to build a lovely high platform — quite square and nice — and there between the three tall pines he painted it green. Then he made a little pair of steps in the rear leading up to the 6x6 foot deck. These too, he painted the only color his brush knew. This was as far as he could go. The following day we drove to the shop of a carpenter some miles away.

Just as I had known that I must have the lifeguard chair at first encounter — so I immediately recognized the "apprentice" to it. Yes, it was its apprentice for I would place it on the new deck and it would sit next to and slightly beneath my present mature chair of prayer and only until I was sure that it was the proper spiritual child to the older wooden one — would I remove the first one forever. And so it was bought and taken back to the lake and lifted up onto its platform and then scrutinized from below by me. I liked its appearance. The true test, however, came in the using of it.

I climbed up and for the first time sat in my hard slatted natural wood Adirondack chair. It was wonderful, and the slant of the high back rest was perfect for night prayer — for lying my head back and gazing up at the stars and the moon through the tall pines. The curved front of the seat was perfect for my legs. But it was those arms — those wonderful wide arms on the apprentice that made me see the possibilities at hand.

It was on these arms that I could not only place my own — but I could place my books, my writing materials, Rosary, pens and camera. I could be comfortably surrounded by all that I might need at any given moment. This was truly a special feature for I never went down to the lake without at least seven books — just in case I might need the other six — my journal and large legal pads, my favorite pen, and the camera and Rosary.

In the past I had had to contain all these necessities in a big canvas bag which I lugged with me and which I could barely carry up the flight of steps. Once up I would slip the canvas handles onto the slender arm of the green chair and feel the comfort of these treasures near me. I would rumble about in the bag at intervals searching for the next project — often dropping things to the ground below. Many thought me strange — but this was where I was closest to Heaven — in spirit, height and in pursuing my interests.

Now — here in my Adirondack — I could have all my belongings out in the open to gaze at and appreciate and if one should fall accidentally from the arm it would drop to only as far as the platform beneath. There would be no climbing down to the ground to retrieve it. Yes, this one feature of the lovely broad arms would place the apprentice in good standing and hopefully help the old familiar chair to be more readily released and retired so that the new one might begin its service.

And so the days passed — the old master standing tall just outside the embrace of the familiar trunks of the three pines that had confined it these long years and the apprentice upon its deck in the honored position that once was the master's — just slightly lower in stature in height and being. Only time and use would reveal if the position could be maintained. Day after day I climbed into the Adirondack utilizing all its features in my prayer life and solitude — and feeling content — but still I allowed my old friend to remain close by me. Only occasionally now — to be fair to my new chair — did I sit in the old.

And then came the moment that can't be explained when I knew in my heart at last that my precious prayer chair of long standing could be put to rest and its title passed on. The apprentice had served by the master's side for sufficient duration and now had earned the right to be the only prayer chair by the lake. And so it was!

The final crowning was the coat of green paint it was given by that famous brush — a sign of total acceptance and of family membership. I lovingly made it my own by my continuous presence within its large arms. My prayers gave it holy blessing and honorably charged it into official duty and service — and so perfect was this new chair that the old one was not mourned — only fondly remembered forevermore.

And so extraordinarily comfortable was its structure that in due passage of time and use I realized that it was worthy of being much more than just a seasonal chair of prayer. I must have a counterpart in my prayer room in Pennsylvania so that in all winter seasons of all the years to come I could in spirit feel that I was by the lake and with eyes closed visualize the view of water, clouds and tall pines and the hum of the boats going by.

No soft recliner or over-stuffed sofa did I want in my room. I wanted to experience within its walls the austerity of a monastic cell and the most modest of furniture. Through such surroundings I drew close to God just as the New Hampshire beauty and nature brought about the same spiritual fulfillment — only more intensely.

And so the Adirondack that had surprisingly replaced the beloved old lifeguard chair was further honored. It was so pleasing to my Monk-heart that a twin of it was purchased and transplanted to Pennsylvania and with a warm brown mahogany stain put upon it — it was placed in the blue and white cell that it shared with a small writing desk, a large bookcase and a lovely altar table of matching brown.

It was the ultimate approval to desire only the Adirondack for my chair of prayer — no matter what the season or state. The old lifeguard master could never have had its duplicate brought to a room in Pennsylvania, for it was one of a kind made years ago and ridiculously out of place unless by a water's edge. In my sad and loving surrender of the old chair for the new — I had been given the spiritual joy of the aura of the master complete with wind and sun and night air and birds and crickets visualized and experienced in a realm of another dimension. My beloved high chair had bestowed on me the lasting gift within my spirit of lake and woods and prevailing winds that I loved — through my willingness to let him depart. Only through the adoption of the apprentice could I transport a precious corner of my outdoor world I cherished in New Hampshire to a small enclosed room over 400 miles away. My Adirondack was the outward symbol of a spiritual legacy I would forever hold within.

And with these memories came flashbacks of both joy and suffering experienced in my chair of prayer — of times I had rushed there in happiness and praise — and of times I had rushed there in tears and defeat. I closed my eyes and turned to Jesus in thanksgiving for His Presence and strength through all those times past — the good and the bad. I needed Him now more than ever. He drew me to Himself. When next I looked out upon the lake it was dark and the moon was on high.

Part Sixteen

"The Lord will give His angels charge of you to guard you in all your ways"
— Psalm 91:11 (Revised Standard Version)

Back in the darkened cottage I turned on several lamps and the brightness that came forth seemed to represent the light that had been given me while resting in Jesus by the lake in prayer. Part of my darkness within had been flooded by His light and love and I felt I had in some way been given new help and strength and a measure of healing of heart and soul. And there was joy and a bit of hope that wasn't there before. I picked up little Chester hugging him to me and then enthusiastically described his dinner to him as I combined his vitamins — a mixture of five important elements that I mixed myself at the advice of a well known author and cat authority and stored in cans to have always ready for each meal — with his prepared Mixed Grill canned food. He had waited patiently for this dinner delayed by several hours and as I bent over the table stirring and mashing and telling him how delicious it was he ' utted his little forehead into mine repeatedly in love and appreciation. Serving it with a flare and another hug for him I had to restrain from cuddling him instead of allowing him to eat. It came to mind instantly at that moment when I was finding him so irresistible that Our Blessed Mother also loved him dearly. There is a little legend that is such joy for me to think on because I have always believed Rochester was sent directly from Heaven to me — a gift from Jesus — and this legend reveals just how precious he truly is. In America and other Christian countries my little breed of cat — a short haired marmalade tabby — has this legend of his own. It is said that as the Christ Child lay in the manger, no animal — not even the gentle little donkey or the faithful sheep dog or the rabbits — could soothe the Tiny One to sleep. But when a little orange or golden marmalade cat jumped lightly into the manger and began to purr a lullaby — the little Babe fell asleep at once. Ever since all tabbies' foreheads have borne an M in token of Mary's gratitude. It is a very evident marking in the fur of Rochester. When I pointed this out to my family after learning it they just sighed and teased believing I was looking for ANYTHING that I could attach a religious meaning to in regard to MY little cat!! Bob topped it all by saying the M stood for Methodist! That was fun — and clever — but Rochester and I knew he bore the mark of MARY. I left Chester to enjoy his meal and boiled water for tea and prepared my Lean Cuisine. While I slowly enjoyed this delicious meal Chester laid by my side and joined me in watching "I Know Why the Caged Bird Sings". Even in movie viewing as in my reading — I preferred films that were autobiographical or biographical or with a strong message — and this film surely touched my heart — and tears as usual came in the experience of sharing this author's life.

More reading, letter writing and updating the journal — all causing late hours again — but intentionally and prayerfully I was trying to delay sleep — and the beginning of my last day of solitude. My fears of the hours of dark and being in the night alone were still with me but, despite the fears, I had risen above them and not let them defeat me. Prayers were still said and books read and writing accomplished and thinking done in the silence and stillness — even though I was wrapped in blackness beyond the drawn drapes and curtains and I did not have the courage to peer out and see the reality of it. To know it was there and neighbors were not was all I could handle.

But surely this had to mean SOMETHING — that I lived through it night after night and was able to function and exist AS IF the sun was shining instead of the moon. That surely meant some healing had been taking place and a measure of fortitude had been implanted in this otherwise extremely apprehensive hermitess. And what is more I would do it all over again — and longed to remain — so that had to mean some delicate work of His was being conducted in this very nervous being despite myself.

William James the famous American psychologist has an interesting thought he calls his "AS IF" theory. He states *"The voluntary path to cheerfulness, if our spontaneous cheerfulness be lost, is to sit up cheerfully and act and speak AS IF cheerfulness were already there. If we act AS IF from some better feeling, the bad feeling soon folds its tent like an Arab and silently steals away. Emotions would respond from the motions"*. In other words — in going through the motions we get ourselves prepared and in gear for the emotions that we desire.

In my case then — each evening I was acting cheerful and AS IF no fear was present or even the blackness of night that caused the fear. Perhaps in the refusal of actually looking at what enveloped me outside the cottage one could say I was like an ostrich with his head in the sand avoiding the issue — but for me this worked along with my prayers — and I was able to cope — AS IF New Hampshire knew no nightfall. I also knew it was a circumstantial fear — for all through the years when here with my family, I was on the outside peering in night after night while they were all in the security of the well lit cottage laughing and reading and playing games. No fear was in me at those times as I sat for hours in the dark in my prayer chair by the lake. I had perfect peace and not a crackling twig or chirping cricket or anything that stirred in the woods brought unrest. Those sounds were all part of evenings spent under the stars. The reflection of the moon on the water was a sight to behold — even causing a poem to rise within me in one particular period of prayer.

It was the realization this week of knowing I was ALONE in the woods that brought fear and yet I knew I was truly never alone. I thanked Jesus for giving me the courage not to give in to it and for making His presence known to me in so many ways.

William James impressed me in earlier years also when I came across a quotation by him concerning writing and journal keeping. It inspired and spurred me on in these endeavors and I entered the quotation in the front of each blank book I began as my own journal and in each blank book I gave away to others to be used as a journal. Along with quotations by Thoreau and other journal keepers that I inscribed on the inside covers — always I entered the wisdom of William James — *"The greatest use of life is to spend it for something that will outlast it."*

And so I did go gently into the night AS IF it did not exist and with eventual sleep. But the morning I wished would never arrive made a sunny appearance — forcing me into my last day of Retreat and the eighth anniversary of my Mother's death.

Frozen lake, Lake Balch. Scene from my window.

Part Seventeen

"For those who have been faithful, O Lord, life is not ended, but merely changed, and when this earthly abode dissolves, an eternal dwelling place awaits them in heaven"

— from the Burial Mass

"Eternal rest grant unto them, O Lord, and let perpetual light shine upon them."

My Mother's death had come as a shock. In fact it occurred on the very day that we were to have brought her home from the hospital. A week previous to that my daughter Jessica and I had taken her into the hospital after receiving her call that she was ill. She had attended a Christian Business Women's luncheon and felt symptoms of illness there. We drove to her home in Olney — a community on the outskirts of Philadelphia where I had grown up and ten to fifteen minutes from Jenkintown. We found her sitting on the front steps of her attractive row home in a lovely pale green pants suit. She always looked snappy and up to date and enjoyed clothes and jewelry — oh, not the expensive sort of jewelry — but the fine costume jewelry that she had worn and created for years as the manager of a busy costume jewelry store in center city — just one store in a large chain.

We helped her into the van and drove to Germantown Hospital and gave her over to those attendants in the emergency room. After a long wait we were told by a physician that she indeed had a heart problem and would have to remain in the hospital. This frightened us — but we left her there and returned home

91

to give this full report to the family and to engage others to pray for her as Jessica and I were already doing.

I felt that she had been stricken in this way due to a very sorrowful year that we had all shared with her. The previous August my Dad, known to others as Ellis George Gray, had suddenly died — absolutely breaking her heart and ours also. He had been a wonderful guy and loved by all. We had all missed him terribly. Two months after his death my Mother found her only living brother, Elmer McKay, dead on the floor of his living room. When he did not arrive to pick her up so that they might go out to Sunday dinner together — she phoned and phoned. Receiving no answer she phoned his neighbor who had a key to her brother's home and the neighbor learned my Uncle's state upon entering his home. My mother took a taxi there and found her second heartbreak in such a short period of time. I will never forget that day as Bob and I joined her there to make arrangements for my dear Uncle. She and he had been a part of a family whose parents were born, raised and married in County Antrim, Ireland and then came to the United States where they in turn had a family of nine children. Several had died in childhood but the ones who lived to older age were fine men and women. My mother, Violet, had been the youngest living for many years and she and her bachelor brother were extremely close. He went everywhere with my Dad and Mother and often spent evenings with them in their home. And the three of them were frequently in our home. For her to lose both these men in her life in a period of two months — took its toll upon her health. Though a strong Christian — her emotions were frazzled and she kept herself busy — too busy — in the emptying of her brother's home and the dispensing of his belongings, while remaining involved in her church and other Christian activities. We attempted to help her in his home but she would refuse our attempts. It was as if this deep involvement was a form of therapy for her. She became easily upset and irritable at times but we knew why her moods were such as they were. We insisted she come to New Hampshire with us over Thanksgiving so we could surround her with fun and love and new sights to enjoy. Just the long trip in the van proved to be wonderful to her and once here on Higher Ground she seemed to be truly higher in spirit.

Constantly when not into these other activities or matters pertaining to these two sad and sudden deaths and of her Methodist Church — she was crocheting and knitting scarves and shawls. Beautiful pieces of needlework were created day after day and even while in New Hampshire she made several items for our daughters. I remembered now too, all the treasures that were found piled behind two large recliner chairs in her den — the den she shared with my Dad for television viewing and conversation and for doing her handwork. Following her death we discovered dozens of these beautifully crocheted and knitted scarves and shawls and each was lovelier than the other. This too, obviously had been her therapy — to release her feelings through the creation of these colorful items. Slowly through the weeks ahead we gave away many of these handsome pieces to her family members and close friends and others in her church who enjoyed her friendship. She would have wanted us to do this for she herself was a great giver. I kept a number of scarves to put away for the future so that I might give them to yet unborn great grandchildren of hers. At the time of her death she had only one infant great grandson — two month old Stephen Daniel Hudson. And I know to this day that her creations live on, and for that I am happy, because so much of her inner being had gone into the creating of each little stitch. Alone in her den who could say how many tears had fallen upon the yarn as she steadily worked and made these heirlooms as a release.

But she had loved being with our girls and George in New Hampshire that Thanksgiving of 1977 and my daughters told me later that she slept with the picture of my Father and Uncle under her pillow. She had shared this with them before sleep the first night.

Once back from New Hampshire she returned to all she had been doing before and suddenly had to be hospitalized for her heart following a checkup. She had never been seriously ill before and was a young looking and active woman in her early mid-seventies. This came as a surprise! The physician warned her to slow down — but she went back to all her responsibilities of my Uncle's estate and refused to let us help except on two occasions of moving furniture from his home to hers in our van and for the dispensing of his many wonderful books in his library.

These deaths had not been her only heartbreak to cause this physical breakdown. On February 23, 1977 — the February before my Dad's August death — an Ash Wednesday and the first day of Lent — my Dad had had to have his larynx removed due to cancer. He had smoked all of his life and though he made attempts to stop — he had never achieved a permanent freedom from this addiction. This was a most strange operation and a very depressing and depleting recovery period and there was much tension between them. My Dad had remained in the hospital a month — all during Lent. Bob and I prayed for him and very strictly fasted — to support him while he remained on liquids. Dad's personality changed because of fear and frustration — and having to write notes to my Mother and to us for each thing he needed to express. She was with him constantly for she, too, had fears. He was depressed and sad and we often found her to be the same. Just when he began going to a special school in the summer and was beginning to learn to speak in a new way from deep within himself — he died suddenly of a totally different problem — peritonitis. How well we remember him saying our names for the first time in this new manner of speaking. He was so proud that he could. Each name was a great effort. I will always remember my last moments with him as I kissed him goodbye — not realizing it was the final kiss. As I left his hospital room — the same hospital in which my Mother died — he watched me leave and when I turned to look back at him he raised his one finger on the bed side he was grasping — indicating a wave. He was too weak to raise more than a single finger or attempt to use his new faint way of speaking. It took great energy to speak. His energy was gone. He died several hours later at 1 AM August 21st, 1977.

And then came Tuesday, September 19, 1978 and the call I received to take my Mother to the hospital. Always I felt that this happened due to the occasion. This was her 50th wedding anniversary and the first anniversary without my Dad. She remained in the hospital for almost a week and Sunday, September 24th, we were told we could come for her on Tuesday the 26th — one week following her admission to the hospital. Monday night I had been to my Catholic Charismatic Prayer meeting at Chestnut Hill College and there we again had prayer for her. I came home believing she would be happily out of the hospital next morning and in our home for a brief recovery period. She had refused to live with us following my Dad's death because she was active and independent. We honored her decision. We could barely get her to agree to stay several days with us after being dismissed from the hospital.

I had come home from the Prayer Meeting and after talking with Bob I began to read. Shortly after midnight a call came from the hospital instructing us to come there immediately. Her blood pressure had been dropping steadily and they did not think she would live. How similar was this call to another we had received in the early AM of August 21st, 1977 — this call from my Mother to say my Dad had just died. She had been the one to receive the call from the hospital. I cannot express my emotions at the time of this second call. I could not believe it was happening again.

Bob and I rushed to her side where we found her connected to monitors and other machines. She could not speak to us nor did she see us — but the nurse said to continually speak to her for the hearing is usually there. And so we talked to her and told her we were right by her and that we loved her — and as we did we watched the line on the monitor slowly flatten and die away. My Mother had gone to Our Lord and we were again in disbelief over a sad and sudden passing of someone we loved. In the interim between my Dad's and Uncle's deaths we had also been shocked and deeply saddened over the sudden death of our good friend, Bill McLean. He had been one of the pall bearers for my Dad and one month later he was gone after cutting his grass — at age 52. These deaths affected me more than I had known and in the months to come I would need prayer and spiritual direction. My Irregular Person was "just that" through all of these deaths — completely "irregular" — and following the last of the four — my Mother's death, there came confrontation from this one and spouse of this one that deepened the pain not only in myself but in Bob also.

We had a glorious Praise and Memorial Service for my Mother in her beloved St. James Methodist Church and she wore for the occasion her new lovely black and gray dress that she had gotten just for my Dad's funeral and then wore once again for her brother, Elmer's. She could not attend Bill's services. They had come too swiftly after my Dad's.

The week of her 50th anniversary I had planned to take her out to lunch for the occasion. I could not do this on the actual day due to her commitment to her Christian Women's Group. Alone with her at this time I would have told her of my prayerful decision to enter the Catholic Church and confide to her all that had led up to it in my spiritual journey. I would have told her that my instructions with the priest would begin October 11th. I felt she would understand despite my Methodist upbringing for she knew I was intense in my spiritual life and in my reading and she totally approved of my being part of this beautiful Catholic Prayer Community for the past four years and often wanted to just sit with me so I could share spiritually with her. She loved all the little holy cards I gave her and at one time asked me to buy her a large supply — an assortment. She then began giving them to people in her Methodist Church and they were touched and appreciative as she had been to receive them. And so I felt in my heart she would understand my decision. She had experienced the support of my Prayer Community when my Dad and Uncle died — for many Mass cards were sent to her and a large group came to the viewings and services. This touched her so deeply.

Because I never had a chance to speak to her about my decision to become a Catholic — on the night of her viewing and service there in her Methodist Church before her casket was closed and the service began — I slipped a little Irish one decade Rosary into her hand as my earthly way of telling her that her daughter would soon be Catholic. I chose this sort of Rosary with its lovely green beads because she was an Irish girl. She already knew this news as she looked down from Heaven — but it was something tangible I had to do for myself as an outer symbol of the step I was about to take. It was necessary to share it with my Mother. She was buried with the Rosary in her hand and with other little keepsakes we tucked in beside her.

As I grew more at peace in heart and mind and as my Catholic instructions progressed — it came to me that my Mother had given me a gift also as I prepared for this new step in my life. Her very last words to me on this earth on the Sunday two days before her death as I said goodbye and left her hospital room were to tell me that she had a present for me. She instructed me to go to the back bedroom in her home and there I would find a white suit hanging on the doorknob of a closet. I protested as I always did when she tried to encourage me in the matter of clothes but she insisted and overrode my objection. "Please take the suit" she said — "you will need it for something special".

Had Our Lord given her spiritual insight before her hospital stay? I will never know. But I obeyed and took the suit. It was lovely and a perfect fit and with a new black sweater I purchased — I wore the white suit for the first time December 13, 1978 — the night I was received into the Catholic Church. Because I did not share an interest in clothes as my Mother did — often to the point of disregard — as often happened she had gotten me to wear something she had selected. Even after death she had made certain I would have the finest of outfits on this most miraculous of occasions. It has often since made me smile when comparing it with so many other incidents in our life together. She had had the last word as usual and made sure her daughter was properly dressed — because she knew she could not be present in person to influence and insist. Other daughters reading this perhaps will smile also recognizing similar relationships with their own Mothers.

And so as this last day of Retreat and solitude began — I took time to remember my mother — Violet Gray — a little lady whose name was most colorful. And all through that day she was with me and I knew she was helping me and seeing my problems in ways she never saw them on earth for I had not confided them to her or my Dad. She knew only about my Irregular Person and not about the ongoing ripples of heartache that stemmed from that source — and so her advice was consistently loving in order that peace might always reign.

After much pause I dressed and then feeding Chester I left him to go outside to my prayer chair to make my Spiritual Communion. How I longed to be at Mass this special day. Following my prayers I drove to the Post Office and found four letters waiting — written by three in our Muffin group. Once again I was blessed to hear twice from Ruth and now also from my faithful friend Olga — and from Mary — encourager and well known Christian writer — an inspiration to my own writing. I carried the treasured mail to the Nest with me when I went for coffee — but let it remain unopened so that I might have it to read and savour later at various times throughout the day. What would this last day alone hold for me? Soon I would know. I trusted Jesus to bring some resolutions to my concerns before I would next encounter Bob.

Part Eighteen

"When people do not respect us we are sharply offended;
yet deep down in his private heart no man much respects
himself."

— Samuel L. Clemens

In the restaurant I had read the two letters I received at the
Post Office from my friend Ruth. They were encouraging and
loving just as she always was to others and myself — and now
at home I read all four letters, rereading Ruth's, with Olga's and
Mary's. I was indeed blessed to have this group of friends who
shared my faith and love of the Eucharist and other interests that
enriched our spiritual lives. I was appreciative for the time these
three friends had given to me.

I opened the sliding front doors so that the breezes could flow
in. The day was not nearly as warm as the day before that I had
spent outdoors — but not chilly enough to have to be pent up without fresh air. The lake was a brilliant blue and glistening in the
sun and the wind blew the waters into little choppy whitecaps.
I sat on the sofa and prayed and Rochester climbed up, circled
about on my lap and laid in a little round furry heap on my lap.
How could the day not be fine with such a loving companion.

It seemed to me after prayer that I should finish the book that
Jesus placed in my path the first day of Retreat. This still continued to astonish me each time it came to mind — that after
pausing to pray in my rented car while Bob left in the limousine,
that Jesus should cause this urgency within myself to buy my
son-in-law a blank book for a journal instead of urging me to
center in on my own aloneness and Retreat. How strange He

should send me shopping in a mall instead of to the woods and silence. I thought back again on how I headed straight for Walden's and even had to wait until the store opened. And when I entered, immediately on the second aisle of new arrivals of non-fiction this book stood there in spiritual neon lights. Jesus drew me to that store and practically handed me that book so that I might not waste one moment. He desired that I find out why I am so depressed and hate myself and lack confidence. I came to this place apart with no self worth and He caused me to discover this book within the first half hour of my Retreat. He knew there were so many areas in my life I wanted to tackle in just these five days that I was given alone — and I saw now that it could not be done. But by showing this book to me at once — He set me on a slightly different course and a very unexpected one. He decided to reveal to me that my past HAS influenced my present and that is why I am as I am. Had I not read this book that Jesus presented to me Monday morning I would still be confused and wondering about so many difficulties. This book took me back to my childhood to show me why and who I am at this present moment and then into past relationships since my childhood. Jesus was there as I learned in these pages that I simply cannot just wipe away the past and forget everything that occurred. Never having professional help and not wanting to confide in others in order to protect those in my life — I depended solely on my own prayers. Deeper prayer of inner healing has been needed and perhaps by one other than myself. Sometimes we are so immersed in and affected by our inner conflicts and pain that we just never pray effectively for ourselves and should call on another who has deep spiritual commitment to our Lord to do this for us. I have — with the help of Jesus — helped many others in the past through prayer and by being actively involved in a healing ministry — but all the while I remained with my own problems within — not wanting to reveal them in order to show love to the ones wrapped up and involved in these problems. I never wanted these ones to be seen as less — or hurt — for I truly believed that was indeed un-Christian to expose ones you loved. This caused confusion when disagreements would arise — for then I was often told by one close to me that I am unforgiving and bear grudges, if I would become upset or depressed over something in my past. This made me feel then LESS a Christian — but I could not rid myself of the causes within that would not allow me to forget, for I guarded these secrets believing it to be the Christian thing to do. It was an unending circle and I know I contributed to my own problems and pain. I was guilty.

But now in this week Jesus opened my eyes to bring me love and peace and then firm knowledge that I was not confused or unbalanced and that it is not wrong that I am not yet right; that it is not wrong that pain and memories cannot be wiped out and forgotten just because someone says that they must and should be. I know now it will take much courage and deep prayer to bring about the resolution to problems in this area — and I know already through my own inner promptings from the Holy Spirit — I have taken steps to be stronger even before this Retreat. But with the wisdom in this book that I never before knew or could call by a name — and with the help of Jesus — I pray believing that I can *"forget those things which are behind and reaching forth into those which are before — I press toward the mark for the prize of the high calling of God in Christ Jesus."* (Philippians 3:13,14)

The Holy Spirit too — reminded me of a saying a priest of our parish had mentioned in his New Year's day sermon and I had recorded. *"Do not forget that which is worth remembering. Do not remember what is best forgotten."* Though excellent advice it was not always possible to achieve — but certainly through the healing power of the Holy Spirit it could — in time — be realized. Jesus indeed, gave me new understanding through the pages of this author's book and I decided that it was this book I must finish this last day while alone and also allow time for rereading of certain sections. Oh yes — *"In the woods we return to reason and faith."* Emerson told me that! And so with my violet covered tea cup filled to the brim and my faithful Rochester bedded down on my lap — I read — but not before becoming lighter in spirit

just at the sight of that cup for it reminded me of the giver —
friend Rose-Beth. She had written that she had been too involved
in outside activities and that now she was going to remain at
home more with her animal companions Nora and Buck, slow
down, and make time for reflection. Her Mother had called this
"getting a grip on yourself." Yes, that was it! At last — in His
love and power — and in His woods — I was GETTING A GRIP
ON MYSELF...

Taken on Retreat in New Hampshire.

Part Nineteen

"For I know the plans I have for you, says the Lord, plans for welfare and not for evil, to give you a future and a hope."

— Jeremiah 29:11

With my reading in this book completed I went outside to roam around and think and examine pretty stones and just enjoy the unbelievable scenery of brilliant foliage surrounding and reflecting in the very blue lake waters. I took more pictures and then climbed into my prayer chair for deeper prayer and to be enveloped in wind and sun and transported into Him.

An hour passed and though I hated to part from my platform — I climbed down to go back in and to write more in my journals and to think about my goals. I read the Bible also and Jesus lifted out a passage of scripture from Jeremiah that gave me hope — one I never recalled seeing before and so perfectly meant for this period — but my mind kept returning to the book I had just completed and about my past — and then to wondering what I would do first in the present concerning this. In reading books by other women I find I am not alone in so many of my thoughts and concerns — particularly about the past. Alice Koller's soul searching and soul baring made me see this intensely. I can quote an unknown source in speaking of her "Unknown Woman" — *"A certain book has turned up and approached me as a friend would."* This I can say of Alice's wonderful book.

Liv Ullman — the well known actress and author wrote her heart thoughts down on paper and the result was an intimate book of revelations from her deepest being that could only help others in their child-like simplicity and utter openness. She titled it "Changing". She quoted another woman author as saying... *"There's a young girl in me who refuses to die"* — and Liv herself then confesses: *"I live, rejoice, grow, and I am always struggling to become grown up, yet, everyday because something I do affects her, I hear that young girl within me. She who many years ago was I. Or who I thought I was."*

And I say "yes, yes" to this. Indeed — our past does deeply affect our present and our future. And how many times I have thought to myself since my six children are all now grown and only several remain at home — or said seriously, yet with a smile to a friend — "What am I going to be when I grow up?" I feel as if I, too, am always struggling to become grown up and to be someone that Jesus can be proud of — an individual and my own self as He intended me to be and not just someone's mother or my husband's wife. I want to achieve the dream He put in my being to write for Him — to be a real writer of worth so that I might help others as I have been guided and helped and directed through my long years of reading. "I hear that young girl within me" also — the young girl who always loved to write letters to family and friends and wanted to become married and have six children; six, because she had grown up lonely as an only child and much was expected of her. Jesus had allowed a great portion of her dream to be fulfilled with fine husband and six children but now — in this time of HER "changing" and having daughters marry and leave home — what was she going to be when she "grew up"? Would He at last allow her to be used as she desired and write for Him? Would He bring healing into all these areas of her life so that she might be whole and with confidence — and not a weakling and a door mat or one described well by a close woman friend and confidant when she scolded her loudly one day with "Jan, you're afraid to take up space on this planet!" This was said in deep love and friendship — from one whom I've shared with and trust and who in turn trusts me and has received my help. She knows me and cares about me and there-fore felt the freedom to blast it out in discouragement when she again saw my own discouragement and meekness and fears.

Words of Liv Ullman's were ones I understood and could claim as my own also when she states that everyday she tries to write but that it is so difficult because of the telephone and her child and many interruptions. She continues that if she had been a man all would be different because a man's profession is respected much more and also the work he does at home and his fatigue and his need for concentration. But she goes on and writes — *"Try telling a child that Mamma is working when the child can see with his own eyes that she is just sitting there 'writing'."* Liv sits and writes until bad conscience drives her from her place alone into the life of her family and she is polite and acts as if she had all the time in the world, but inside she is angry that she felt the need to stop writing and make an appearance. She feels like a bad mother and makes excuses for everything she is doing because she knows that her child and others cannot understand why her writing is important to her. She is afraid to put music on as she writes lest her family think she is loafing and she realizes that all these are her thoughts and "female guilt" as she tries to write about how good it is to have a life that gives so many choices and so much freedom. She states that to feel respected she must produce pancakes and homemade bread and have neat tidy rooms.

It cannot be written any more clearly than that regarding my own life. These are some of my exact problems and guilt. I can be writing alone and hear someone enter the house and I jump up to look busy elsewhere so they would not mistake my writing for idleness. I am embarrassed because of my personal areas of clutter because when I write I make a mess and am surrounded by books I love and paper, and then I shut doors to hide all of this. I feel guilty leaving it like this and it hangs over me as I write, but because my writing time is limited then I choose not to use that time for cleaning and straightening. Eventually it is mentioned — my awful clutter — and I'm confronted — and I feel like that little girl again that is inside me receiving my scolding.

All of this I share with many other women and, though I was a

college graduate and a trained Dental Hygienist, married and raised six children taking full care of them and spending much personal time with them and giving them a spiritual foundation as well and also at the same time keeping my home pretty and clean without the help of a weekly housekeeper that so many of my neighbors had, and working all day every day on a Christian tape ministry in my home for seven years without monetary benefit but spiritual blessings to the heights, I now felt I had no purpose in life and certainly not the respect of my family who now saw me as a Mother with grown children and too much time. My writing was seen as a hobby to them or nothing at all. I was even told that now it was time for me to concentrate on being a grandmother. I am still young and I did not want to concentrate on being a grandmother and that does not mean I do not love each one of my grandchildren. But my first grandchild was born when my youngest child had just turned nine — and eventually they were even in the same school system together. I am still a mother and not quite finished being one — and my youngest is only seventeen as I made this Retreat — and I do not want to begin all over again and concentrate on caring for little ones once more. I want to be with them and love them and know each one so carefully, but they cannot be my life as once my children were and are, with my activities and desires restricted or sacrificed in love according to their needs and lives. That was joy to me to give myself to husband and children and I still do — and to stay at home to be with them — but now that little girl in me wants to continue along her journey and I know what I want to be when I grow up while remaining open to even further guidance — and it isn't only to be a grandmother! I must follow that calling that Jesus put within me just as I followed the calling to enter the Catholic Church. Pope Paul's quote held meaning for me — one that I had recently entered into my Commonplace Book for affirmation and also confirmation to my own inner feelings. He said: *"In the design of God every man is called upon to develop and fulfill himself, for every life is a vocation."*
How many women are there in this world that can identify with

Liv Ullman's confession; *"I have spent hours completely involved in what I thought other people wished to see me doing. The fear of hurting, fear of authority, the need for love have put me in the most hopeless situations. I have suppressed my own desires and wishes and, ever eager to please, have done what I thought was expected of me."*

Now — as I sat in deep silence thinking these thoughts — I realized I must make definite goals, and for me that meant writing them down. Out came the small journal meant for this Retreat alone and I prayerfully began to list objectives that would be starting points for me to help myself to change and as I committed myself to these few and became stronger — I could branch out a bit further into others. My very first goal was to begin to use the help given to me within the book Jesus had given to me the first half hour I was alone on Monday morning. My second goal was to set aside a scheduled time each day to write, letting nothing interfere with this unless it was urgent — treating my writing as a job. If I continued in my special ministry of writing spiritual letters of encouragement to others that I believed Jesus gave to me and that I've been told so often by friends and recipients of the letters that He has indeed given me this as a gift — and if I kept my journals faithfully — then perhaps this step of faith into a disciplined routine of writing would make me more open to the next special things I believed Jesus wanted me to write for Him, but that in my depression and fears I have blocked out and been unable to hear or to receive in prayer.

If I am serious about my writing then perhaps in time others will take me seriously considering the importance of it to me. To Thoreau his journals were his life and his life was arranged about them in order that they might be beautifully kept.

My third goal was to continue to be disciplined in eating and to continue to lose weight, for I knew myself and that to be the least bit overweight makes me self-conscious and feeling less a person. Childish perhaps — but at this point still necessary for me if I was to effectively help myself change.

Goal number four — which should have been listed as number one — as it is listed in my heart — was to continue in disciplined prayer — more time in front of the Tabernacle after Mass to be with Him and more prayer times alone at home in my prayer room. I must defeat my fears and continue the work along these lines that He began within me this week. Only prayer would wipe out the fears and give me the courage that was given to me in many instances while on Retreat. I would use an old prayer form of visualization also — seeing in my mind's eye the "FIN-ISHED ME" — and having already achieved these goals with the help of Jesus. This is faith, believing in light of Hebrews 11:1 that says: *"What is faith? It is the confident assurance that something we want is going to happen. It is the certainty that what we hope for is waiting for us, even though we cannot see it up ahead."*

And lastly, though I felt self centered thinking it — yet remembering the pain and wounds and many awful incidents in my past — I wrote that I would try not to think of myself as being so bad an individual. If anyone — and especially those that have repeatedly done so before — behaves badly toward me I will remember that the behavior is THEIR problem, and I should not let them place that on me to make me feel worthless. I should not have to accept the blame for another's irrational behavior — succumbing as in the past as they place on me the very things that are really their shortcomings in anger and rage and false accusations. Help me to remember Eleanor Roosevelt's quote: *"No one can make you feel inferior without your consent"* — and let me see these individuals as ill ones who won't accept their inadequacies and try to change. Let me recall the principal messages of a passage I now read frequently from a devotional book that my friend Pat had loaned me to take on this Retreat. These words advised: *"Let me not take to myself, and suffer over, the actions and reactions of other people"* and *"God teach me to detach my mind from what others say and do, except to draw helpful lessons and guidance from them."*

Since this sort of situation has caused some of my deepest pain — I knew this goal would be the most difficult to achieve. But He had shown this week I was not a NOTHING and that I had to be stronger. I would be now, with and in His strength and with the aid of goals one, two and four. And for me, I also need goal three until more firm in the others.

I sat back and relaxed and reread a passage I had written earlier in my journal by Thoreau. It seemed to tie it all up for me.

"I learned this, at least, by my experiement; that if one advances CONFIDENTLY in the direction of his dreams and endeavors to LIVE the life he has IMAGINED, he will meet with success unexpected in common hours."

He had learned this in his Walden when he went to the woods and I will take special note of that word CONFIDENTLY. Jesus has given me new confidence in my Walden experience also — so that I may advance CONFIDENTLY in the direction of my dreams.

Thoreau concludes this passage by saying: *"If you have built castles in the air, your work need not be lost, this is where they should be. Now put the foundations under them."* As a Christian — my foundation would be more prayer — disciplined prayer — and trust in my Lord Jesus Christ.

I would recall also and reread and record in my journal the passage from scripture Jesus had pointed out earlier from Jeremiah — as I faced both unexpected and anticipated life changes. This verse proclaimed that God is in charge. God does mean well for us. God plans for us to have a future and a hope. My prayers this day would also reach out to all others in transition and to all who suffer change and seem to be in a "strange place".

I looked suddenly at the clock and saw much time had gone by and so I quickly straightened the living room of the cottage where I had spent most of my Retreat, changed my clothes and placed Rochester's food out — and hugging him with the promise of my return I left to drive to Rochester and meet Bob.

Part Twenty

"Without your love Lord — my life would be empty
Easily filled by the forces of sin
My need is constant — just living depletes me
My heart is open, Oh dear Lord come in."

"Give me the strength Lord, to follow your teachings
Help me to see through life's folly and greed
Then your goals for me will be my objectives
You are the Savior, the Lord God indeed."
— Robert A. Kolb Jr.

It was dark now as I left and drove out our dirt road through the woods and onto the small Sanborn Road that in a moment joined the winding Route 153 — a scenic country road that led through borders of fall foliage and views of small ponds. In daylight it seemed almost as if I was under an archway of autumn trees alive with color on the trip to Sanbornville and Mass at St. Anthony's — but only headlights provided the necessary light now and none of this beauty was seen.

This too — was another first for me — to drive alone here at night for any distance. Driving is something I enjoy and I drive great distances when in Pennsylvania to parts of the Delaware Valley that others in my family never tred nor are familiar with in any way — and in New Hampshire I am also the one who goes about in the van more. There is frequently shopping to do, errands to run, post office to visit, Mass to attend and I have always been the one to take my daughters on outings — especially when they have brought friends along from Pennsylvania and we have wanted them to see a little of the area. But any night driving — unless to the local store — was never done without a family member along — for there are no overhead lights on the highways or country roads. To drive the roads was not what frightened me for I did it regularly. To have the van stall or stop altogether or break down in any way and be alone in the dark — was my greatest fear.

Often when we have come home late at night as a family or just myself with several of my daughters — we would pause on our dirt road in the woods and turn out our headlights. There was utter blackness. I have never seen such blackness! It was not much better on the larger roads or highways — unless one would occasionally see headlights of a passing car. So if the van failed and one was alone — Ah, horror of horrors — one would either have to stay within it with locked doors until hopefully family missed you and sent someone out to find you — or one would have to walk for help along the pitch black tree lined wooded roads. Think of the trauma to one's emotions in either situation! Gas stations are miles apart and there are very few homes. THEREFORE — I even hesitated to make a quick run to the local store for any reason, (though I have) — unless some one accompanied me — for our mile long dirt road in the woods was the darkest of all. If the van ever died there I probably would also. Sending help to me would be useless.

But this night was different. I did not know myself! Perhaps it was my week of Retreat and staying in the woods alone that gave me confidence — along with having a brand new rented car that was unlikely to break down instead of a van that could not always be depended upon. But I drove the forty minute — 18 or 20 mile trip in the night and felt at peace. Mixed emotions were within. It would be so good to see Bob and to express again my appreciation for his great part in delivering me to the woods — but I also was not ready or willing to leave. I was still trying to deal with this — to find peace of heart about it — as I had just discovered I had about night driving in New Hampshire.

Walden's was included in this trip. I had hoped to end my Retreat in the bookstore and to actually thank Jesus at the very spot in front of the shelf that held a supply of the same book he had drawn me to Monday morning and lit up in His love. But I misjudged the time believing the mall closed at 9:30 PM instead of 9 PM — and that portion of my plan was not complete. However I did stand outside the mall and touch the back wall of Walden's and offer my thanksgiving to Him.

The restaurant and its parking lot where the limousine would deposit Bob after its run from Logan Airport in Boston was only five minutes away. Driving there I parked the car under a giant overhead light, one of many that surrounded the parking lot — although none at all were on the streets. Pulling out my small portable journal that I always carried I wrote and prayed alternately for the next hour and a half — being able to see perfectly in the light provided to make my journal entries. As I sat with closed eyes a rapping came on the car window that jolted me incredibly! I'm not one that takes unexpected arrivals calmly whether in full light in my home or at night in a parked car — so that jump was my normal reaction and Bob knew it would be. However — knowing no other low-key way to get my attention he tapped the window.

Following our reunion he drove us to a nearby Pizza Hut for neither of us had eaten. There over pizza and coffee he brought me up to date on happenings in Jenkintown and I was able to share just a few surface incidents of my days alone. The meal was delicious and, both subdued, we drove the miles back to the woods with very little conversation — this time with him at the wheel. Rochester awaited our arrival in happiness.

Part Twenty One

"For He that is mighty hath done to me great things; and holy is His name."
— The Magnificat of Mary
Luke 1:49 (King James Version)

Another day dawned cool and fall-like and because no food was in the house due to my limited and controlled eating, Bob decided we would eat breakfast and dinner out at the Nest. This would be a nice finale to my week. We left for the restaurant and enjoyed our time there, all the while sharing together happenings of the past week. My new acquaintance was there — the waitress who had waited on me in past mornings — and after greeting us, she entered frequently into brief conversations with us. As we were leaving she showed me a picture of her six year old son and then told me in confidence the results of the tests done on her nephew the day before. It was a sad diagnosis and I promised her my continued prayers and thanked her for her support and friendliness — for just her "being there". It was not a final goodbye for the winter. We knew we would see each other again soon in October and November.

Returning to our cottage we found our neighbors there, Dennis and Patti, up from their home in Massachusetts and outside and waiting to greet us. A friend of Patti's was also there and we invited everyone for coffee. Soon we each went our own way enjoying the outdoors. I continued to take pictures and tried to finish up some reading to complete my Retreat — reading in my prayer chair while Bob did some of the maintenance that he enjoys doing on our grounds. The day passed too quickly and soon it was time for the drive into Sanbornville to attend the 4 PM

Mass. It was wonderful to be there — to end my week of solitude with Mass and to be able to thank Jesus in church before the Tabernacle and to receive His Body and Blood. It was the ultimate way to draw my Retreat to a close and to prepare myself for going back to Pennsylvania. As I drove Route 153 back to the cottage, inwardly I was strongly resisting my return to civilization. Anytime I am forced to leave New Hampshire it is disconcerting and upsetting to me — but on this last day of this significant week it was more so.

As I drove down our dirt hill to our cottage Bob was waiting. After feeding and hugging Rochester — Bob and I went again to the Nest, this time for a relaxing dinner. Many were there and it was good to see the main room filled with people from E. Wakefield and surrounding areas I loved. Often, teasingly, as we sat in that crowded little restaurant at dinner amongst both the townspeople and seasonal vacationers — I would stretch out my arms and say to Bob — "This is my place and these are my people". Very few we know personally but there is such a loving spirit existing that I just experience affection for these folk and their friendliness. It is just a good feeling within to realize that they all share a deep loyalty and fondness and love for the Wakefield area and the lakes and the woods. We are among kindred souls and one can almost reach out and touch that "warm feeling" that exists. It is further evidenced by the smiles and hellos from strangers and the patient waiting for a booth or table without impoliteness. And so we enjoyed our favorite meals — specialties in our favorite restaurant — Bob's of meat loaf and mashed potatoes covered in gravy with Russian dressing salad — and batter dipped haddock and plain mashed potatoes with blue cheese salad for myself* — and always with wonderful coffee. We pass up their many delicious sounding desserts. Due to the generous home-cooked portions we can never complete the main course. Dessert would be impossible.

Before leaving I selected two pins from a display card on the counter. They were small black and white replicas of the Common Loon — a bird protected on these lakes by the residents with

---

*Bob and I have both since become vegetarians for the sake of the animals! (NOT for the sake of diet!) We do *not* eat any meat, fish or poultry!!

faithfulness and pride to prevent them from becoming extinct. I had noticed the pins earlier in the week and one was for myself to mark this period in the woods. During my Retreat I had several times seen a loon out on the water in front of our cottage diving and crying out his plaintive wail — in deep water and alone like myself. This little pin would be a keepsake of this solitude. The other pin I would carry back with me to Jenkintown to give to the young woman I did not know except through loving remarks and instances shared about her life by her mother, Ruth — who was one of my ''Muffins'' from daily Mass. All during my own Retreat I had remembered the love this young woman (also Ruth) had shown to me in the days previous to my coming to New Hampshire in allowing her Retreat of some years ago to be shared in order to encourage me to go to the woods alone.

My friend Ruth had related in detail how the younger Ruth had gone on a three week Ecumenical Retreat in Colorado with a 20 member group led by the ''Christian Outdoor Leadership School''. The first week consisted of a base camp; with all activities centered there including talks, classes, and the learning of songs. Hikes were also taken but the hikers always returned to the base camp the same day. This first week was to establish community — creating a bond for the two weeks that followed.

The second week included more hiking plus back packing and making camp in a different place each night. All of their belongings including tents and food were placed in a large pile indicating it was now up to everyone there to share the load. This procedure then made every person totally dependent on each other and all dependent on God for their survival. So many selfish little incidents occurred that caused annoyance to the group. Even what might seem a small one under normal conditions of one person eating all of the crackers as a snack — was a major annoyance to all involved when dinner was to have been tuna fish and crackers. With no bread or cracker replacement — tuna was their total meal.

The third week, however, was one of endurance and particularly affected Ruth. A portion of this is what she wanted to emphasize to me. The week began with having to run for ten minutes without stopping at various intervals, and the high altitude made it more difficult. This was more physical exercise than Ruth could do and so she would walk at times to complete it.

Then came an experience that she had never undertaken before — far more overwhelming than anything so far completed in this camp — or at any other time in her life. It required an inner spiritual strength that would be tested as well as her physical stamina. The group was tied together in order to climb a mountain and the slowest people were put in front. She was frightened and found it extremely hard to keep up — but she forced herself to climb — step by step — clinging to rope and rocks. She began crying softly in fear. She found it all unbearable and her physical strength failing.

Suddenly through her tears she saw something shining in a bush. Reaching into it she took hold of the object and drew it out. It was a gold cross! A miracle! Her spirits leaped and she interpreted it as a sign from Jesus that He was with her in this ordeal and was lovingly protecting her on the mountain and in all that was to come. It brought to my mind when this was related to me of the beautiful song we sing at Mass — *"And He will raise you up on eagle's wings, bear you on the breath of dawn, make you to shine like sun, and hold you in the palm of His hand"*. Surely He could not have made Ruth shine more brightly within or show her more clearly in her fear that He was with her every moment. She continued and completed her dreaded climb clutching the cross.

Once upon the mountain each Retreatant was assigned an acre of ground and each was to camp in the middle of it. She spent the night in the pitch dark alone with nothing but her Bible, poncho and flashlight — and only once did her leader come by to check on her condition. She felt the "peace that passeth all understanding" as she held the gold cross in her hand — knowing she was being cared for and watched over by the loving Lord. She was able to pray and fast and be restful alone with Him there and to feel His presence. He banished her fears. She finished her

Retreat in a new and deeper relationship with Jesus — and inwardly she had been spiritually strengthened. His "Sign of the Cross" had left an indelible imprint upon her soul — and now on mine in every recollection of her experience. Ruth asked her mother to tell me of her Retreat and in every detail to encourage me to go to my dark acre also. She knew He would overcome my fears and that He would give courage and signs of His Presence.

And it had been so — and I was ever grateful I had not turned my back upon this gift of time alone. He had called me to the woods — just as He had done to Thoreau and Alice Koller and so many others before me — and I had responded. My "yes" had been life changing. He came to change human beings — even the most ordinary and common of us into new creatures. Jesus Christ IS the Changer! His first miracle on earth — the changing of ordinary water into the finest of wine at the Marriage of Cana — signified His true mission among men and His true nature. This first miracle established His ultimate purpose — His eternal purpose — which is to effect changes in the hearts of men and to lift us from the lowest of depths to the highest of heights so that we might be made into the sort of person who will forever glorify God in his words and deeds and bless the world. And though He is the "Changer" He has given us the assurance in Holy Scripture that He is the "Changeless" Christ — that He is the same now as He was 2,000 years ago and He is present to work miracles and He is concerned about our existence. Yes, *"Jesus Christ, the same yesterday, today and forever"* (Hebrews 13:8) was a scripture verse I loved and knew since childhood — and His constancy should be forever a comfort and strength in our lives.

This young woman Ruth had dramatically experienced His concern about her life and her fears there on that mountain, and she "took up His cross" and more deeply followed Him from that moment on. And because her dark acre held a place in her heart and burned within her in a special way — her darkness became a light for me on the path to my own dark acre. We would forever pass the light from our darkness onto others. He knew that we would and so this little Loon pin would be given to her as the outer symbol of all the love and gratitude I felt within for her and for her deeply personal encouragement to me.

Once back in the cottage Bob went to bed at 8:45 PM in order to obtain sufficient sleep for the trip back to Jenkintown. Our plan was to leave by 1:30 AM. I changed into more comfortable clothing for travel but I was not ready to go home. I wanted to stay longer alone to try to get myself completely together. There were yet too many unfinished areas of my life not yet touched upon that remained troubled. I felt like only a quarter of a person. I needed to become whole again. Rainer Maria Rilke has been given a spot in my Commonplace Book with his comforting remarks that I frequently read: *"What goes on in your innermost being is worthy of your whole love; you must somehow keep working on it and not lose too much time and too much courage."* Thoreau had approximately two years in the woods and Alice Koller had four months alone on the wintry Nantucket — Five days alone was not enough! It was surely better than nothing but only the beginning of this journey. Fears were still with me, the greatest being the return home and the fearfulness that I would go back into the same depression and tears and the extreme feelings of uselessness and inadequacy.

And so I spent my last hours alone in quietness and prayer and in reading favorite excerpts from Thoreau and other significant authors — and in making some final entries in my journals. Rochester spent these hours next to me with occasional moments of stretching and returning to my lap where he had first begun our evening. I prayed fervently that Jesus would help me as this week of solitude ended and to keep the memories of this solitude in my heart and mind to call upon and draw from in time of stress and worry and depression if they should come. I prayed that I might be momentarily carried off in spirit to this same precious solitude, again to feel the refreshment and joy of being renewed and alone with Him and with my Communion of precious saints — as if in reality — as in these present moments and in those of the past week.

I was going home "in faith believing" yet with fear too — if that is strange to see next to faith — that Jesus would use "this week" in my life to give me strength to face all the "coming weeks" of my life. I had to believe that SOMEHOW and in SOME WAY I was different and that this time alone had indeed MADE a difference. I had to remember that Jesus Christ is the Changer!

I was not less a person because I was not like others with greater achievements or worldly successes. He cared about my existence and was changing me according to His plan for my life. I had said "yes" to His gift of aloneness in the woods. Like Mary — the handmaid of the Lord — my desire was to always give Him that "yes".

I reread a passage from Thoreau that held meaning for me and encouragement. *"If a man does not keep pace with his companions, perhaps it is because he hears a different drummer. Let him keep step to the music which he hears, however measured or far away."*

I would continue to listen to the music of my "Drummer" — Jesus Christ — and step to His music that led to "Higher Ground".

Picture of "Prayer Chair."

Part Twenty Two

"Accustom yourself to unreasonableness and injustice.
Abide in peace in the Presence of God, who sees all these
evils more clearly than you do, and who permits them. Be
content with doing with calmness the little which depends
upon yourself, and let all else be to you as if it were not."
— Francois De La Mothe Fenelon

And so I left the woods in New Hampshire journeying back
to whence I had come. All would be the same upon my return.
Each situation and difficulty would still be in existence and would
not have changed. But I had changed — or was in the process
of being changed by the One Great Changer — Jesus Christ —
and therein was the difference. I had forever as my own — this
week alone. It was mine — to return to in spirit to gain new
strength and courage from whenever needed. It had been given
to me by Him as a new beginning and turning point in my life.
As we three drove in the new white Cutlass Supreme, Bob, myself, and Rochester forever on my lap — it struck me that He
had even made possible that I would have this rented car for
the week. Driving it had given me a feeling of being a different
person. It was new and strange and I was alone in it. All of that
was so totally opposite of the norm. The large van had been removed from me for the week that was a symbol of family. It represented many things back home. It also could be unreliable at
times. It was as if He drew me out of all of that — home, car,
failings and dealt with me as a single individual and not one who
was part of a unit. He gave me His undivided attention — something He always gave to me but I did not feel worthy enough
to ever believe that. He made me feel like a person — a "Cin-

derella" perhaps — and the lovely white car was my "pumpkin chariot". He was allowing me to feel my own personhood and at the same time was lifting me out of the "rags" of depression and despair and discouragement and "clothing me" in the delicate garments of Himself — in His peace and healing and love. And He was helping me to put on the whole armour of Christ as revealed in Ephesians 6 so that I might come against the wiles of the devil and not be brought down into the rags again found in the emotional gutter the evil one had been dragging me through. Even this revelation concerning the rented car was proof that my heart and mind were healing and I was thinking beautiful and encouraging thoughts and not ones of continual self disparagement. There was a long road ahead but I had long ago chosen "the road less travelled" and suddenly I realized anew it WOULD "make a difference". When first I chose this road it was like the path to Heaven for my conversion to the Catholic Church had been fulfilled on this road. But I had allowed the evil one to plant tangles and thorns that wrapped around me and pulled me down in the dirt. I had the empowerment of the Holy Spirit within me to do him battle but I was so worn down from the thorns of people in my life I had trusted and situations that had become tangled and overgrown with weeds of despair that I had given up. I had let the devil walk all over me through other sad episodes and through people I loved and cared for deeply — and I only limply fought back. I protected those I loved who deliberately hurt me so that others would not see their dark side and double nature. At times I had drawn comfort from Psalm 55 — wherein the Psalmist cries out in despair that it would have been easier had it been someone he barely knew or did not like — but ah — his soul friend — how could his beloved friend have done this? It was like death! (verses 4-5). All he wanted to do was run away. *"Oh that I had wings of a dove! for then I would fly away and be at rest. Lo, then I would wander off and remain in the wilderness."* — and for me — this meant flying to the woods of New Hampshire! Part of him wants the one who has wounded him so to be hurt in like manner (verse 15). He simply still cannot believe it — they had taken *"sweet council together and walked unto the house of God in company"* (verse 14) — what fellowship they had — what wonderful discussions! — Then the hurt was delivered so sweetly — smoother than butter. He cries out *"This friend of mine betrayed me — I who was at peace with him. He broke his promises. His words were oily smooth, but in his heart was war. His words were sweet but underneath were daggers"* (verses 20-21) — *"It is not an enemy who taunts me — but it is you — my companion, my familiar friend"* (verses 12-13) Oh — this truly is anguish of the worst kind! How well I knew this anguish! And each episode and problem the devil used to drag me down further.

Not anymore! This week in the woods could not be in vain. It had to be forever the outer symbol of the inner change that had been afforded me by Our Lord. And if I did not begin to live out that change and will it in my life then I would be ungrateful for all that He had given to empower me.

We are told to love the sinner but hate the sin and I had obeyed this — but often I had loved so much that I had permitted the sins to be repeated again and again against me. We must turn the other cheek and forgive 70 x 7 — but is it not giving the devil recognition for a Christian to allow another Christian to continually abuse him and use him? I was a sinner also — for ALL have sinned — but He had given me the grace to keep pressing onward and trying to change. I was always aware of my sinfulness and unworthiness. Apologizing again and again in order to make relationships right was perhaps a weakness in myself and even invited trouble. To be righteous and unbending and never wrong as these loved ones were and never saying "I'm sorry" after humiliating and displaying anger and betrayal — was evidence that the devil was surely present. Often I had become terrified inside in these encounters for I truly felt the evil one in the atmosphere and saw it in the eyes. It is said man's eyes are the mirror of the soul and have great power. When God dwells in a man it is very evident, for his eyes carry God to men. And when the evil one has a man in his grips the eyes are blackened and intense and there is an iciness and chill that comes over the individual that has been confronted by such a personage and fear mounts within uncontrollably. Horribly frightened we then do often not use the powers within us given by Jesus Christ to ward off the evil one. We grovel, cringe — even cry out or perhaps flee — and we have been trodden upon again and weakened by the onslaught. Later we realize what we SHOULD have done and wonder if we WILL when we are stricken again. And we KNOW we WILL be stricken again! We love and care and therefore put up with it. Sometimes the encounter almost seems the best choice when we consider the awful consequence of NOT accepting it and perhaps radically dealing with it and thereby risking the end of a relationship with someone we love. Or perhaps the period of pain we endure, no matter how painful — is more comfortable to us than an ongoing suffering because of having angered the person more by demanding a change. To ride the roller coaster of the individual's moods and know at least there will be heights and plateaus of good and love in the relationship too — between the times in the pits — is often the easier and safer course while we pray that we can change the individual through our prayers. Now Jesus had shown me in this week of Retreat that in allowing Him to change ME was the ONLY way. My "yes" to His gift of aloneness in the woods had shown Him I wanted more of Him and a new spiritual inner strength obtained only by surrender to Him and willingness to be changed.

I had turned my cheek 70 x 7 and forgiven these people over and over because I truly loved them but suddenly I began to see that perhaps my forgiveness was not complete because I had not forgiven myself. How many times after the first or second startling episode of being stricken a blow or having been betrayed did I ask God silently where was His justice? Why didn't THESE people too, experience deep pain and have their heart slain with despair? The Psalmist (Psalm 55) had even gone drastically farther by crying out *"Let death seize them, and cut them down in their prime!"* (verse 15). Why did He see and allow the awful unchristian behavior of these individuals in hidden situations yet let them be seen by the majority of the world as saintly and holy — doing no wrong? How often in deep suffering during or after an incident did I wish that similar pain be given them in the degree they had battered my heart and soul and being, so they would never do it again and so that I would know in the NOW they had been punished and not have to imagine and trust they would have to answer to our Lord at some unknown future time when I would not know. When we are hurting so — our thoughts are not always pure and kind. Our body and soul might act out forgiveness to the person due to our deep love and truly behave in love and forgiveness instantly again even after an onslaught. But when forgiving them did we forgive ourselves? Certainly there are times when we said "I'm sorry, Lord" for that thought — but maybe not sufficiently and completely. Even confessing such thoughts thoroughly in the confessional as I had done many times brought forgiveness from our Lord — but obviously not from myself. Maybe we feel after a while almost deserving of some of the suffering because we believe we are not Christian to have these vengeful wishes. Often when we are used time and time again as a door mat or punching bag by another Christian that is admired in other Christian circles — we begin to blame ourselves and actually become convinced we are being punished for some sin of our past or a sin at the time unknown to us. Our thinking and rationality becomes irrational and we live in a constant state of unworthiness and self-hate and confusion. It is truly a vicious unending circle and frequently the one being betrayed and hurt begins to believe there must be something defective in his own nature — a flaw — to cause others to turn on him in this way — people he loves when all he wants to do is love and be at peace. Unforgiveness of self has many facets and causes.

The Lord made provision for us to be able to forgive ourselves and yet it is certainly true that we can honestly and fully forgive people that have injured us but somehow we can not find the spiritual strength to utilize God's strength to forgive ourselves. At various times in our marriage Bob had brought to my attention when it seemed pertinent, some true events in the life of his friend for whom he served as "Best Man" at his wedding. He was also a member of our wedding party. I thought of these events now and how as a young man right out of high school Bob's friend had entered the service and in the early part of America's entry into World War II — he was captured by the Germans. Formal prisoner of war camps were not set up early in the war though later "stalags" were provided for captured soldiers; Canadians, Americans and all allies such as British, French and Russian. But at the time our friend was made prisoner, existing facilities were used — concentration camps that had been used for Jews and Gypsies. Many Americans ended up in these same camps — though not integrated with the Jews and not in the same barracks. Basically the living conditions were the same for both Jews and soldiers — but the soldiers were not put into the gas chambers. Living conditions, however, were sub-human and unbelievable, far worse than conditions that would later exist in the "stalags" — for they were controlled by the terms of the Geneva Convention agreements.

As a result of the terrible depravation in these prisoner of war camps the disease and death rates were extremely high among Jews and the soldiers and others in this situation. Because of these many deaths there evolved a procedure for taking care of the bodies of the young men that died. They had to be removed from the cell barracks and the deaths had to be recorded, and the recording witnessed and attested to concerning how the person died. This attesting to was done by other prisoners of war.

Certain individuals were chosen for this death detail. They would take the body to the proper place where the papers were processed then proceed with the body to the assigned area for burial. After completion of the burial the soldiers of this detail were given a meal before they were sent back to the prison. Therefore, it soon became very desirable to be put on this detail because in a despairing situation where people were in a semi-starvation condition continuously — one good meal was most important and perhaps the difference between life and death.

And so — as the horror of the captivity increased daily and

starvation became a greater factor — the men would look forward to being put on this burial detail in order to obtain a good meal. Eventually things became so distorted and bad that the prisoners that would be on this detail would feel joy when a fellow prisoner died — perhaps even when a close friend died — because the person would at last be released and freed from this horrible situation through death. But it also meant a substantial meal to those who would take part in processing his records and burying his body. This was a Christian young man who survived this camp and who was released at the end of the war. Although he was able to forgive his captors for the horror he had experienced he was never able to forgive himself for the feeling of satisfaction when one of his fellow prisoners died, because it meant that he might live. He could not see with his spiritual eyes that this feeling had originated through a sub-human existence while immersed in an ongoing evil that he had not physical or spiritual or emotional strength to rise above during that captivity.

At times he became so deeply depressed by his inability to relieve himself of this guilt that he became incapable of functioning in the normal world. He couldn't study, eat or have a social life. He never dated girls with the exception of one that he met much later. He dated only her — and soon after they entered into marriage.

Bob knew him in a period of approximately five years after he had been released and he was still suffering with guilt anxieties at this time. Although he graduated from college with excellent grades the rigors of his professional school studies and obligations were such that it was hard for him to keep up due to depression.

We knew that his depression and accompanying guilt continued for at least four years after this and since we lost the very intimate sort of touch that had previously existed, we do not know if it was ever really resolved. Our hope has always been that he received God's strength to forgive himself. One day we know we will again experience a deeper sharing as before and know the outcome. Long miles of physical distance have prevented this but our friendship has remained intact.

This is only one person's suffering in regard to the inner tor-

ment of not being able to love or forgive self. Also, another facet
of unforgiveness of self often appears while one is still in the
depression and aftermath and confusion of feeling total unworthiness following betrayal.

Once someone uses you or betrays you and you allow it —
then the stage is set for a repeat. Individuals know who will take
their evil nature and who will absolutely refuse it. I know this
to be truth. If that same individual would do to another even
once what he has done to you repeatedly — his holy reputation
would be ruined and cast down. Therefore he is the model of
virtue with the ones who would not stand for insults and humiliation for fear he would receive them in return. His darker nature
he vents on a loved one whom he takes for granted and whom
he believes loves him. This he knows causes even more horrifying
anguish to the one stricken because the person trusted and believed in him. Often it is sadistic behavior. Then frequently later
the abuser's excuse will be that he couldn't help himself — or
that he lost control — or that he doesn't know why he behaved
in such a manner. This to me is not truth for this same individual
or individuals would not ever exhibit horrible behavior of this
magnitude and evil in their office with their fellow workers or
in their church with their fellow parishioners. They are selective
whom they choose to destroy. There is a knowledge of right and
wrong or otherwise the behavior would be uncontrollable in any
place or with any person. In contrast they are often sycophants
to persons in their other environments. It seems the loved one
causing suffering simply has no conscience at the period he
chooses to hurt and humiliate the person who loves him, and
then the evil one is allowed control. Most certainly there is a deep
psychological problem but yet the behavior is only selectively
vented — thereby the victim knows the loved one KNEW what
he was doing and CHOSE to turn on him. After someone has
gone through this with another who has stricken him and they've
allowed it — it almost seems this part of his being is visible and
the individual becomes a door mat and begins to receive blows
from others close to him. It is unbelievable to the one being hurt

— for it is as if he attracts evil and suffering. And the pain is intense for it comes from ones loved and trusted. And the guilt within of causing it becomes a cloud of confusion constantly over the heart and mind of the victim.

A true story was told by a priest in a sermon of a method he had read about used to trap monkeys in Africa. Pieces of fruit that the monkey loves were put into the bottoms of glass jars. When the monkeys saw the fruit they immediately put their hands in the jars and clenching the fruit in their fists they could not get the fruit or their fists out of the opening of the jars. Since they refused to drop the fruit so that they might run and go free — they were encumbered by the jars and easily captured by their captors. Later when alone I reflected — is this not the same with human beings? We often insist upon holding onto loved ones for fear of losing them and destructive habits and guilt and offenses done against us — thereby we are held captive by the evil one because we refuse to change. Change can be frightening. We cannot release all that is keeping us bound. We cannot ''let go and let God''. We cannot open our palms upward to Him in surrender so that He might take all these encumbrances from us. If they are put into His hands and not clenched ''in ours'' we will then be open to His healing — physically, psychologically, spiritually and emotionally. Like Lazarus we will go from death to life if we listen to the voice of Jesus and obey. If we do not we will remain entombed — actually experiencing a death-like oppresion and remain captive of the evil one. That light and spiritual insight came powerfully to me after I had begun to write these reflections about my week in the woods alone. In deep prayer here in New Hampshire one October day last fall — 1987 — I received words from the Holy Spirit — a grace and blessing that is always wonderment to me each time it has happened — and being prepared with pad and pen as I am accustomed to be — I immediately wrote. And this is what was whispered within my being:

''Our Lord Jesus came to give us victory in all areas of life. He rose from the dead and we must see this as the most priceless

gift. He left behind in the darkened tomb the bindings that kept Him bound. He asks us to do this also and gives us His Holy Spirit and His promises in order for us to be set free.

Unleash the bindings of depression that keep you tied up in knots and bound to untruths the devil whispered to you. Listen not when he speaks of your unworthiness, your mediocrity, your ugliness and your nothingness. Unleash those bindings and with a claim of victory declare "It is written" and like Jesus who declared these words before you — you will ward off the snare of the evil one and refuse to let him have any hold on your being.

Mentally and spiritually pull these wrappings of death from your mind and heart and soul and rise up as Jesus did and walk in freedom and victory from the death of all that the evil one would have you believe is yours.

When Christ arose He gave us the promise that we, too, would have life eternal and life abundantly in Him. Walk from the tomb of your particular darkness as Lazarus did. Jesus called him forth and He calls you also. Give Him all your torments and discouragements for He careth for you.

Roll back the stone — in the power of the Holy Spirit — that keeps you entombed in the devil's lies. Surrender to our beloved Lord and Savior and walk out in the brilliance of His love. He will fill your soul with light casting out all darkness within — and you shall know the truth and the truth shall set you free. You shall know our risen Lord!

Let it be said of you also — "he is risen" — risen above the deceptions that held you bound. Show to all that Christ arose by your new life in Him." — (Matthew 4:1-11, Luke 24:12, James 4:7,8, Romans 8:32, Matthew 28:1-10)

And so I was beginning anew my new life in Him — changed by Our Lord — and stronger and wiser spiritually and emotionally. Though occasional waves of apprehension ran through my mind concerning certain awaiting situations and persons at home — I would immediately return in spirit to my woods and lake and solitude as I silently travelled away from it in reality — and peace would come. This spiritual weapon long ago given me by Him when He brought my prayer chair into my life was my treasure. I lived more in spirit than in reality anyway and returning to the woods via the Holy Spirit and imagining within was frequently a consolation from disconsolation long before this "WALDEN WEEK" just experienced. But in my "Walden" this treasure had again been reinforced into my spiritual life for continued peace, healing and comfort amidst the daily trials that would come and the reoccurring heartaches. How faithful He is — !

My interchanging thoughts and prayers continued as we entered the back roads of Hightstown, New Jersey and arrived at the garage where our van had spent its own personal week of Retreat and repair. Spotting it in the lot brought a new rush of reality to my being and though I was extremely fond of the van and enjoyed driving it — it represented what lay ahead and would be the vehicle to carry me back to it all. Again — a wave of apprehension. I no sooner experienced this silently than a police car came speeding towards us on the quiet dead end street where we still remained seated in the rented Cutlass. It stopped abruptly behind us and one of the police officers stepped out and called to the boy in the garage that had helped us the previous weekend. We learned through the loud conversation between officer and boy — that the two young men in the police car with the two officers had been picked up for stealing a van and taking a joy ride in it. The officer was inquiring if a van from this garage had been stolen and the boy had told him "no". The shouting officer roughly ordered the younger men out and told them to lean against the police car. They were then searched — all this happening before us in a matter of mere minutes. In all of this episode it seemed the one disturbing sight that held my attention was the handcuffs. Both boys were wearing them and they were such a contradiction to what two boys should be experiencing in life. In my spirit I realized Jesus was showing me ACTUAL chains and how they bind and constrict and take away outward freedom and inner emotional and psychological freedom as well. I cannot remember the last time I saw chains — or specifically handcuffs — and yet at the very time I was about to reclaim our van and return to situations that had imprisoned me in despair and that had caused me to want to break free and flee to the woods — Jesus showed me what real chains looked like to refresh my memory. He let me see this sadness of being a prisoner — of how the problems in individual lives can truly keep bodies and soul bound and chained. I knew I would begin to pray for those boys that they, too, might one day become un-chained from not only the real chains but also be released from the inner pain and circumstances that had eventually put them into the handcuffs that now held them outwardly captive. Once searched and pushed roughly about — the young men were ush-ered back into the police car and it sped off as quickly as it had arrived. The entire scene was unreal — that it should appear and disappear so swiftly yet be played out before two strangers. I could not even see the boys' faces — or their eyes — I saw only the chains. But I realized it had been permitted by God to happen there and at that moment. He had used an incident already in progress to intervene into my life at the very second I was experi-encing apprehension at the mere sight of our van. In His mercy He was stopping me from slipping back into my former chains.

As if all of that wasn't enough sign of His love, He prepared yet another SIGN. After thanking the boy at the garage for his kindnesses of the weekend before and presenting him with a T-shirt from New Hampshire I remained in the Oldsmobile with Rochester and followed Bob in the van as he drove to the motel where we had rented my car for Retreat. As we three left the motel together in the van after returning my "pumpkin chariot" I noticed the large sign on the winding driveway. In large letters this message stated: "Courage is fear that has said its prayers." Again — that instant "knowing" came in my heart that He had arranged that I should see that marquee. I found it to be incred-ible for in continuing to glance back at it in an effort to keep it in view as long as possible — I saw in rounding a curve that this message appeared only on the one side of the sign. Our side! Had we exited on the other driveway we would only have seen the name of the entertainment appearing nightly in the lounge.

I would never have glanced back at THAT information a second time and would never have discovered the opposite side of the marquee, if by chance that particular driveway even did curve that I COULD see it. And how unusual that a spiritual quotation should be on a motel sign in large letters — given the same high billing as the entertainment of the night life. It was a mystery — and though I called the message to Bob's attention at once and he looked right at it — he did not see what it had said nor can he even remember seeing a sign at all. But I came away with the quote in my heart and there it has remained and in my journal as well. My fears had surely ''said their prayers'' in the woods and the one great changer — Jesus Christ — had changed them into new found ''courage''. How unbelievable that He cared so much that He reached out twice on the last lap of my journey home to reignite that courage given to me in solitude, to fortify me and to let me experience so vividly the power of the Holy Spirit. It is written in the Psalms that Our Lord goes before us and surely He had made this truth known to me.

Upon arrival back as I sat not quite alone in my prayer room (for Rochester was curled on my lap) and felt the Adirondack chair both beneath me and above my head as I leaned back and surrounding me with its big arms — I experienced again with closed eyes — the sights and sounds and smells of the lake and woods. He allowed me this gift of being transported whenever I wished. It was as if the chair was Him — encircling me in His protection and love. I still felt as if an invisible veil or shell separated me from the real world and I wanted to stay within it clutching my week of solitude and all that it had contained. Hesitant to rend the veil by word or action — I remained motionless in His presence in a dimension of wordless prayer and gratitude.

Then suddenly I knew. A knowing came within my heart. It was time to leave my solitude. Forever I would have it in my soul to return to time and again — but now I must begin to live it out in faith — believing indeed, I had RISEN to new life in Christ. I rose from my Adirondack and blessing myself with holy water from the Blessed Mother's font on the wall — I opened the door and left the room. The words of a precious song He had given as comfort to me upon my entering the Catholic Church filled my mind and heart. How often I had needed to hear that song when alone at Mass.

Jesus flooded my soul with it now as I walked downstairs. *"Be not afraid — I go before you always — Come follow me — and I will give you rest"*. Symbolically it seemed — my little Rochester hurried ahead of me down the steps — this little gift in my life from Jesus, even representing Him in a sense — showing me it was time to follow example and see what adventure we would next share as we entered our NEW life.

Cottage, Lake Balch. Wooden cross can be seen. Light on in upper window where I wrote the book.

Afterward

"It isn't for the moment you are struck that you need courage, but for the long uphill climb back to sanity and faith and security."
> — Anne Morrow Lindbergh

Exactly two years have passed since that September day I arrived in the woods for my Retreat. I sit outside now on the dock while the sun sparkles upon the bright blue lake and the strong breezes cause the water surface to be choppy and active. It is a glorious day — a sight to behold — a day similar to those spent here in September 1986. Reflecting back on that week I can only repeat that it was a "gift" and I am grateful.

I know now what I truly could not have known at that time — that it was a turning point. Because I wanted it to be one and because I was thankful to our Lord for this "gift" — I WILLED it to be a turning point once I left the woods — and I WORKED at living as if it was. Accepting by faith that I was BEING changed — I BECAME changed. My fear of failure after being given this "gift" of Retreat was a new force subduing my original fears that had caused me to come away. And that new force caused the turning point. Thank God — for if my life had become unalterable I was doomed. But I can say that good things have happened to me because of my willingness to be changed and to do the very things I had feared the most and to risk the unknown. With prayer and His help I have ceased to let fear control me, though I have not ceased being fearful. I have been given new insights so that I have accepted fear as a part of life and yet keep moving on ahead regardless — despite my pounding heart at times that signals to turn back with a silent screaming "NO".

I have only to return in spirit to the woods via my prayer room Adirondack chair or imagination — or when physically possible by van — and I can "SEE" my turning point. The cabin, the woods, the lake, the prayer chair, the rocks and all the sights and delicious fragrances of nature give that turning point form and reality.

Betrayal and hurt and cruelty He has shed light upon, and the darkness of soul this causes has visited far less frequently. My inner changing by Him made outer relations with difficult people lose control over me. In these two years Our Lord has shown me gradually that if you really understand a cruel or revengeful or vicious self-centered person — you are then entirely free of that person. See him as a frightened person and not as hostile or cruel, for negative emotions truly have their base and foundation in fear and inadequacies. A person exhibits his mean ways according to the depth and degree of his fear. UNDERSTANDING is the key — and then the individual cannot hurt you no matter how he tries. It will not be possible!

Your overall behavior creates an impression of either strength or weakness and as you develop inwardly and allow Our Lord to strengthen and change you — this changes the way you appear to others. There is nothing you can do exteriorly. Strength comes from the inner being to the outer and as your inner self is healed and touched by Our Lord and given new strength and power — it automatically and gradually expresses itself in new forms of outward behavior. People then see you as a different person, for you really are! You have been changed by the One Great Changer, Jesus Christ. And seeing you as a different person you are then treated with new respect. I know. I have learned this. I am experiencing it!

In a spiritual book I long ago lost track of, similar teaching was expressed but I was not capable of receiving it into my life at the time I read it. I was defeated in so many ways. Only after He changed me did I remember this. During this same period I copied from somewhere — from where I do not know — a paragraph called a mental image in order to help me during an onslaught. I am thankful I copied it into my Common-place Book for I have it always to refer to and now to share. It reads: *"Suppose you see a tiger in a zoo. Now you know very well that this tiger is a cruel and vicious animal. He would destroy you if he could. You understand his ferocity, yet you are unafraid of him; his cruelty does not alarm you. Why are you fearless? Because you know he is powerless to harm you. The bars protect you."* I've learned I must see a cruel person in the same way and understand his cruelty. A tiger is restrained by the bars — and a hostile and difficult person is prevented from harming me by my own UNDERSTANDING of him. He has no power to touch me because my new insight of him makes firm, unbreakable bars. However, if I get emotional and personalize his hostility even though it is directed at me — and if I unthinkingly attribute and give power to that person — I am weakening the bars. I give him permission then to hurt me. His cruelty is not my problem. If I don't react in agony and fear toward the cruel person he cannot wound me. Jesus has made me understand this truth — that my UNDERSTANDING of persons will stop them from hurting. The KEY that LOCKS the cages of my personal tigers is "UNDERSTANDING". "NEGATIVE REACTION" is the KEY that unlocks. The KEY OF "UNDERSTANDING" has a dual role. When inserted it also unlocks the chains that kept me bound in despair due to those mean spirited "tigers", that are now caged. The KEY of UNDERSTANDING is another "gift".

That mental image copied four or five years ago could not help until these past two years. I was always uncomfortable with this description of the tiger, for this animal has always appeared strong and handsome to me and the ferociousness spoken of here was due to his being caged and out of his natural habitat. Yet I knew it was an image of truth and it encouraged me to read it. Now that I have the KEY it also enables me to love these personal tigers more. Yes, UNDERSTANDING is the KEY both to LOCK their cages and to UNLOCK the chains that bound me — but my ACCEPTANCE of the tigers just as they are in their unchanged condition is my DOORWAY out of bondage. There is freedom in my soul at last.

For approximately five years I have had a stuffed blue and white cotton print Christmas ornament hanging from my dashboard. Embroidered in its middle is the word "HOPE". It was a prayer reminder — not that I needed one — to persevere in prayer for the difficult persons and situations in my life. I had the dream that I could change THEM. That was my HOPE. Tenseness and restlessness would be always in my spirit as I relentlessly prayed — even feeling guilty if I found myself relaxing. I would cry throughout most of my drives in my car — never ceasing my prayers while the HOPE ornament danced before me. I was tearful and uptight most of the time and things only grew worse. But I always had HOPE and tried to see the good in the person or situation and thought I could CHANGE THEM — so that the good was always there instead of the monopolizing tigers. Then one day after my Retreat my husband and I saw a bumper sticker that made us simultaneously break out in laughter. It read *"Since I've given up HOPE I'm feeling much better"*.

I had been changed and so I knew the real meaning behind this funny quote. I knew the heartache and pain of continuously and intensely trying to change someone or something — of pinning my HOPE on THEIR being changed. Only after my inner change could I laugh at the bumper sticker and myself. Every time the quote comes to mind I have to smile. My friend Ginny who has been a part of my spiritual journey — had the same HOPE ornament dangling from her dashboard. We bought these ornaments in a Christian store one day while together. Depressed and upset over our individual lives and our problems she even personally installed mine in my Plymouth Volare as an act of love and encouragement. Noticing about a year later that hers was gone I learned she had ripped it from her car in a fit of anger and despair. I understood! I hated mine too! Now I'm reconciled with it for it holds new meaning and I let it remain there to remind me of the bumper sticker — and so I'll laugh instead of cry as before.

My Retreat proved to be a doorway into a new phase of living — a transition from living a sub-par life to new inner strength surfacing gradually. Our Lord is subtly changing me and I realize it at times when I least expect. Matters and persons that previously had torn me apart are now not alarming and I face them without my chest pounding and my mouth dry and tears always filling my eyes — and they do not bring me down to the depths. I feel CHANGE and STRENGTH and it is amazing! Sometimes I simply do not even care about the very things that were before my ruin!

A great truth I have learned in my new life is that it is wrong to WAIT for someone else, or to EXPECT someone else to make my existence richer, or fuller, or more satisfying. I had been spending my days, my years always WAITING. It had become my way of life — waiting and HOPING for change. This put me in constant state of anxiety and suspension. To always have to WAIT and be dependent on these unchanged others was emotional and psychological slavery. Worst still, the slightest knowledge of the ''waiting'' to the ones causing it might foster abuse — and did. While in that state I missed all those unretrievable moments that passed. They will never come back to be experienced again.

All this change has not happened overnight and He continues to work that change. That is not to say that I never slip back — but devastation has become a condition of my past. He had gently lifted me out of that utter depth and brought me slowly up through desolation, despair, despondency and disillusionment. I am no longer diminished by my tigers. There is only disappointment. And when I have slipped it was only slightly and momentarily and He has let me see that I will not be destroyed again. When I do not crumble under situations that once broke my heart and spirit I know He is at His work of transforming. It is a continual surprise giving cause for continued thanks and praise to Him for all He is intricately and tenderly restoring and creating within my soul.

While this miracle is in process He has also released me to write. Upon returning home I continued to write my daily letters as I had always done to those that needed encouragement or who were ill in some way — or just letters of friendship. But I was disciplined about it and considered it more important than before. My journals were also kept more faithfully and I began to think of myself now as one who would soon be a writer in a larger way for Jesus if I remained faithful to this writing that I had always been doing. This had been a commitment made in the woods and there grew from it unexpected rewards. In November of that same year while spending additional time in our cottage with my husband, I was at last able to write an introduction to a manuscript of hymns and meditations that Our Lord had given to Bob and me and that one day we hoped we might have published. Many complications had prevented this from becoming a reality and the complications stretched out over a period of ten years. The situations that evolved from this were often a cause of my pain — because again I was depending on someone else and "waiting" and "hoping" — when it was really mine to see through to completion. The loss of the only copies of the forty five meditations was another suffering that went on for over three years until a miracle occurred and my prayers were answered and the meditations were found. But that blessing is told in detail in the introduction I wrote for our manuscript that November day in 1986 and will not be included now for it is a story unto itself. With the writing of the introduction we were then able to prepare and Bob typed the entire work and we prayed the completed manuscript would be accepted by a publisher. It was sent out and in God's time it was accepted and has now been published under the title "Whispered Notes."

Next I took another step and submitted poetry that I had written from time to time and again He answered that act of faith by allowing three poems to be published. Last summer while in New Hampshire and continuing to pray concerning the desire deep within to do much more with my writing, my husband suggested that I begin with short stories — perhaps about our life in New Hampshire and the many things that have happened to our family here through the years. That idea seemed to be immediately confirmed in my spirit so I timidly set about writing my first short story. It touched Bob so when he read it and he gave it such appreciation that soon over the coming weeks I developed a collection of home-spun type stories of life here in the woods. One account I was enthused to set down in written form concerned my week's Retreat by the lake and so it was begun. I wrote and wrote for I found such joy in recording all that had happened. The evidence was soon obvious by the many completed pages that this event in my life was something Jesus wanted written, and that I should just continue until in my spirit I would know it was finished. And so this past year I have written this very story of a segment of my life — a life that continues to change and strengthen — and this release to freely write is further proof that the chains that once bound me in heart, mind and spirit have fallen away. Work on the collection of short stories continues also, and fresh ideas constantly present themselves to be written about and to be included in my "Pine-Cone Journal" — true tales of the special way of life lived out by a lake in New Hampshire. All of this came through this gift of the KEY of UNDERSTANDING — given because I came away in the woods with a willingness and eagerness to be changed. Even now new thoughts for other manuscripts have come to mind and I excitedly look forward to their beginnings — to just write and write forever and for Him.

As for prayer, time had always been seriously set aside for this — particularly following daily Mass and at other times throughout the day and evening in my prayer room. Or if in New Hampshire — then my prayer chair by the lake is regularly used and appreciated. I have on-going conversation within with Him while going about my daily routines. Prayer is my salvation in everything. But in the past two years even my prayer life has changed and deepened. The intensity in prayer to the point of tears that had eventually developed and the stress and tenseness that held me bound were removed. The prayers are prayed now with no less desire and longing — but I am peaceful, with all the terrible tearful striving gone. With fears no longer controlling me I can rest and trust in Him. No cyclone whirls through my system beating me into a frenzy. I am rediscovering *"the peace that passeth all understanding".*

When I am not blessed to be in New Hampshire in reality as I am at this writing — I continue to be transported in spirit via my prayer room Adirondack chair in Jenkintown, Pennsylvania to my solitude in these woods. In pondering a quotation by Ernest Hemingway recently in his book that I reread frequently — realization came that he too — in some way — was also referring to being transported in spirit. I cannot say if he experienced this in a deeply religious sense as I do, but my interpretation after many readings of this book is that there is some indication of "the Spirit" there and that it was not only in his imagination. He wrote: *"If you are lucky enough to have lived in Paris as a young man, then wherever you are for the rest of your life, it stays with you, for Paris is a moveable feast."* He wrote this to a friend in 1950 yet the actual years in Paris he is speaking of were 1921-1926. He wrote *"A Moveable Feast"* long after the years he had lived there as a young man. He began the book in Cuba in 1957 and worked on it next in Ketchum, Idaho in 1958-1959, took it to Spain when he went in April 1959 and brought it back with him to Cuba and then to Ketchum late that fall. He finally finished it in the spring of 1960 in Cuba. It was published posthumously in 1964. Treasuring and remembering this period always — he was able to write about it in detail over 30 years after he had lived it in Paris! This revealed to me that this five year period of his early life of 1921-1926 was always in his heart and had become a part of the fiber and spirit of his being. It was a segment of time that captured and touched his soul. He truly was correct in titling his book as he did for he made the title come alive by the many places he actually carried and worked on the writing of the physical manuscript. It becomes evident that his "Moveable Feast" was not only at these locations with him many years after he lived it — but that it was a "Moveable Feast" always "within" — to be summoned and fed upon in spirit for strength and inspiration. Knowing this has, in turn, been inspiration to me. A little loving tribute I pay to him through the wearing of a Hemingway sweat shirt bearing his caricature. It was given to me by my daughter Barbara and husband Frank to be worn while I write. Daily you will find me in it but only during my hours of writing. God has also made quite clear and specifically shown me since my Retreat that He sees all and that His justice is meted out in His time. Those who knowingly and intentionally break the hearts and spirits of others are NOT spared similar despair in their own beings — and darkness of soul is eventually theirs also. Our Lord has said *"Thou shalt not kill"*. To slay one's soul and spirit can cause a death comparable to and even surpassing physical death — for the stricken one is left to try to survive in this deep suffering put upon him. But Jesus is there for the cruel ones too, if they are willing to be changed — if they say their "YES" — as well as for the ones that were stricken by their evil.

As for that goal of an exercise program — it consists mainly of concentrated work-out of right hand and wrist and the eyes — as I daily answer His call "to write". Eating problems He has not centered in upon either — for my heart and soul were utmost to Him. All other matters I know will be changed in His timing also. Through denial and common sense (most of the time) my daily diet is small. As I await further instruction I have continued to find that one proper meal a day — with occasional exceptions and occasional liquid — is quite adequate. Quite comfortable, really. Any more and tiredness takes over. Eating less then means less sleep is required. My mind stays alert longer and those quiet night hours into the early AM have always been incredible to me even before my Retreat. I pray and think — write and read — or simply "be" in the stillness. With no interruptions! To be able to stay awake is a gift. Though I do not take advantage of this gift every night it is a blessing to know it is there. I realize I have the mistaken view that sleep is a waste of time — and this terrible "punishment" I'm inflicting upon my health with these late hours is regularly and lovingly pointed out to me by my loved ones. While they await the crumbling of my body and senses (several say the senses have already departed), these night hours continue to bring a special "something" into my life. They are peaceful and quieting. They are strengthening — not debilitating. And He is there!

There too — is my little one — my dear little Rochester. *"Whither thou goest I will go"* has to be the maxim Our Lord gave to his little heart from the Book of Ruth as the Holy directive from the Bible for our lives together. Where I am there he is also! Night and day! He has been a little golden gift of pure love for me from Him and every day I am eternally grateful. I agree with the writer Theophile Gautier who has stated — *"Who can believe there is no soul behind those luminous eyes!"* Of that I am certain — not only because of the bond I share with this precious little one and the many acts of his extraordinary love that are demonstrated repeatedly — but because this truth is confirmed in my own soul even had I never read one word of the scriptural evidence.

He has travelled back and forth from New Hampshire to Pennsylvania an estimated fifty one way trips in his short two years and three month life with us, never moving from my lap while travelling. Always upon arrival in New Hampshire there is a definite spirit of happiness upon him that's not there in Pennsylvania. It cannot be ignored! He recognizes this little spot of Heaven! He knows his "Walden".

Just two weeks ago during his checkup the unsmiling veterinarian took some blood for a test concerning a strange new disease affecting the immune system of cats because Rochester had a periodontal problem. The scaling of his teeth and my daily brushing of them would be the normal future preventative for not having the problem reoccur. However his negative words — including the despairing prognosis if Rochester should be found to have this disease — plus his dismal appearance left me shattered and in tears for several hours. Suddenly that inner strength rose up and I made a series of drawings for a form of prayer that I believe to be powerful — that of visualization or imagery. Drawing a test tube of blood upon which I wrote "CHESTER'S PURE AND PERFECT BLOOD", I surrounded it by a beautiful heart with a flame. This represented the Sacred Heart of Jesus and I had placed my Rochester's blood test within it. In the HEART I wrote — "O Sacred Heart of Jesus — I place my trust in Thee." One drawing completed I then made three or four others. Out came the crayons and the drawing became colorful and noticeable. Placing one by my picture of Senor de Los Milagros (The Lord of Miracles) in my prayer room in Pennsylvania — I knelt down before both pictures many times an hour repeating the prayer written within the Sacred Heart and "thanking" our Lord IN ADVANCE for the good news that WOULD come that indeed — Rochester's blood was perfect. Visualizing and imagining the completed and desired good results and backing it with faith is an incredible prayer and based on the scripture of Hebrews 11:1. *"What is faith? It is the confident assurance that something we want is going to happen. It is the certainty that what we hope for is waiting for us, even though we cannot see it up ahead."* Bob and my daughters and son and daily Mass friends prayed also with the aid of my drawings. Just creating the pictures in my hours of crisis had restored my courage and faith. A four and a half day wait was before me until the doctor would call with the test result. My prayers proceeded faithfully in this manner.

During this period I sent a close friend of ours a note with one of my drawings of the test tube within the Sacred Heart. He was a man of prayer and though I had never asked him to pray for a little animal before, my love for Rochester motivated my request. I just knew I could count on our friend.

The afternoon following the morning my note came into his hands — we found under our front door knocker a typed paper — neither signed nor in an envelope. Bob read the first line and handed it to me. Taking it to a quiet place I began to read and with the reading came tears and the knowing that it was written in love from his prayerful heart by our busy lawyer friend who took time out immediately to comfort my heart. These tears sprang up because the unsigned typewritten message was like an epistle from Heaven confirming my faith that all was well. I include it now for others who share their lives with a beloved animal companion or companions that they might see its sweetness and consolation and simple trust — and even for those who do not personally have an animal friend. Just reading it causes compassion for animals and perhaps even a rethinking of our re-

lationship to God's creatures. For me — it is a new and personal
assurance and prayer from Our Lord through my friend that He
is with me in every way in every day — and that trusting Him
is my only hope. Here now is this precious message.

* * * * *

Musings on the Sacred Heart of Jesus — and Pussy Cats

Jesus Christ, son of man, was all man as well as all God.

*When Jesus ascended to be with the Father He ascended with the heart
of man, a human heart. Thus a human heart became part of the God-
head, a heart like ours, that has lived and loved and experienced joy,
pain and grief just as have we.*

*You may be assured that Jesus loved pussy cats and all the other pets
and animal companions God gave to us to delight our hearts and give
us companionship and comfort.*

*It is not silly to pray for a pussy cat. It is an act of trust and faith
to ask our Father to cure our sick pet and enable us to continue to delight
in our love of His gift of the pussy cat. Remember, if His eye is on the
sparrow, you know it is also on your pussy cat.*

Therefor:
*Father in heaven, through the human heart of Jesus, hear my prayer
and make my pussy cat well, for you know full well the anguish I experi-
enced when I consider that he may be taken from me.*
In Jesus name, Amen
— Daniel T. Deane Jr.

When the phone rang four and a half days after the appoint-
ment and the expected call came through, I confidently picked
up the receiver and heard the monotone voice of the veterinarian
tell me Rochester's test came back "negative". Thanking him for

calling and giving witness to prayer — the dreaded moment had turned into one of confidence when the actual showdown arrived. But it does not end there, for a thankful heart is pleasing to our Lord and the personal commitment of five decades of the Rosary each day in thanksgiving for Rochester's health and our Lord's reply — is my gift back to Him forevermore to the Sacred Heart of Jesus who loves pussy cats.

Our Lord is not finished with me and transformation will continue. The healing and the changes are on-going for this I pray. Awareness of the great need for my faith in Our Lord never leaves. As I glance at my little $2.97 watch that has remained on my wrist since my Retreat, it indicates it is time to bring my reflections to a close. Looking now at the large wooden cross on the front of our cottage from my chair by the side of the lake — realization comes once again and with joy that He has truly set my feet upon "Higher Ground".

Rochester

Healing Steps to Higher Ground

"I'm pressing on the upward way,
New heights I'm gaining ev'ry day;
Still praying as I onward bound,
Lord plant my feet on Higher Ground."
— Johnson Oatman, Jr.

There may be those reading this book who need the touch of God upon their lives in a very evident way. Perhaps there are readers whose hearts are broken or spirits impoverished or imprisoned by onslaughts encountered in their individual lives. These Healing Steps then that follow are merely a brief summarization of points written about more fully in the preceding pages — points that will maybe help another to find peace of soul once again.

When we repeatedly experience pain it indicates a need to pause and take a long look at ourselves within and without. We should examine our lives and our own behavior. If we are honest we may see a change is necessary. It may be a change in attitude or a change in a specific situation. Perhaps a change in a relationship with someone or ones — or in some instances an entire turnaround so that we are travelling in a new direction. Continuously experiencing pain and anguish is a warning signal that is often deliberately ignored. Many of us prefer and submit to the pain and remain in it because it is familiar. We would rather exist in this manner because we at least know what to expect. Usually more pain. To contemplate change becomes more frightening than the present suffering — even long term suffering — for by now our low self esteem and poor self image have also robbed us of all self-confidence.

We must come to the decision however, that it is time for change. When we can sincerely make this admission and if we will turn to God — He will meet us as we begin to travel the road to change.

These Healing Steps to your own personal transformation are briefly and simply stated so as to be significant. Often when our hearts ache and we are in pain we can only grasp the uncomplicated and so these directions come in that form. Think of them as handrails of support along your upward road to healing. They come with prayers for each of you — that soon your feet also may be firmly planted upon Higher Ground.

#1   Admit that you need to change and that you have been helpless to do it yourself.

Once this admission is made do not waver from that moment on. Continue to admit it to yourself. No longer agree to remain in the pain.

#2   Believe that God can work that change and bring healing and sanity.

Actually say or pray a simple sentence such as — ''O God — I place my trust in Thee.'' Repeat it frequently.

#3   Surrender yourself to God.

Tell Him that you are placing your life in His care. Say your ''Yes''.

#4   Solitude — Go apart.

You may not be able to go away for several months as did Alice Koller, or even for a week. But in some way create for yourself your own personal ''Walden''. Be it a weekend alone or even a day — make a definite and special beginning to your road to change so that you can be entirely alone and so that that beginning is always carried in your heart. This is most important! Even thirteen years before my Retreat when all six of my children were still at home I began the practice of setting my alarm for 4 AM to have quiet time with Our Lord. I would spend until 6 AM with Him then return to sleep until the family woke at 7 AM. The alarm was not needed eventually. He woke me in my spirit. I continued this period of solitude for years. This can be another alternative for those with children who cannot go away or be alone uninterrupted for even one day. Our ''Retreat'' MUST GO ON after the initial beginning. Time alone with Him each day is essential. But to have a significant ''beginning'' that stands out from all the committed time that will follow is recommended, for it becomes a precious turning point to refer to often.

#5 Listen to Him.

Spend much time just ''being'' in His presence; sitting quietly. Every moment spent ''being'' is a healing moment. Soon you will come to recognize the inner voice — His voice — deep in your heart. He will comfort and direct you. Obey Him. You will begin to change.

#6 Keep a journal.

From your first day apart with Him on ''your Retreat'' write in your journal. It may be only one sentence at first — but write. Your journal holds the record of your spiritual journey and self discovery. It is a release and a confidant to help you understand more about yourself. Write freely. Journal keeping is enforced reflection. When we commit our thoughts and observations to writing we are taking what is inside of us and placing it outside of us. We're holding a piece of our life in our own hands where we can look at it and meditate on it and deepen our understanding of it. Write! Write! Write! — and choose a blank book that is pleasing to you and that attracts you to it frequently. If your preference is for plain pages instead of lined ones then use what YOU like to write upon. Pick one with a cover that calls to you — designed or plain — but a cover that makes the journal irresistible to ignore. I would make only three definite suggestions. First, do not pick a small book, for then you will write smaller thoughts and feel confined. Choose one in size not under 5x7 inches. And secondly, I feel bound books over looseleaf books are preferable, for once you pour yourself out on the pages — the pages remain in the book to refer to again and again — good or bad! You would be less inclined to rip a page from a nicely bound book. Every written page is there to help you on your spiritual road to change. A looseleaf page is too easily destroyed in an impulsive moment and later regretted. Thirdly, never consider writing your thoughts on mere scraps of paper to be stored away. They will be lost and your journal will not be consecutive.

#7 **Pray** and **Meditate** regularly.

Offer your "yes" to Him — your continued desire for inner change. Create an oratory within your soul — or if you wish — a spiritual room or home. Visualize it as you wish it to be in every detail. It is your place of peace and contentment. It is always with you and even when you are in the world involved in duties — keep returning to your "special place" for refreshment and communion with Him. This will change you and strengthen you. Continue in this way ALWAYS what you began in "your Walden". This step of prayer and meditation when practiced has exceptional power to shed light on all the other steps.

#8 **Set Goals!**

In daily close communication with Him they will be achieved.

#9 **Help Others.**

Once you are experiencing your transformation, gradually begin to be aware of opportunities to help others. Listen to Him in prayer. He will lead you to the ones He desires you to help. It is by doing and exhibiting our strength that our strength becomes real.

#10 **Thanksgiving** and **Gratitude.**

Thank God repeatedly each day for all He has done and will continue to do in bringing about your change and healing. A thankful heart is pleasing to Him. Make little personal hidden sacrifices in gratitude for His great love for you and His healing power in your life. Never cease doing this. His healing is on-going!

Katherine Mansfield, the very fine writer who often talked to Our Lord when recording entries in her journal and who was given the strength to write even in her serious illness, wrote some time before her death — *"I want, by understanding myself, to understand others. I want to be all that I am capable of becoming. This all sounds very strenuous. But now that I have wrestled with it, it's no longer so. I feel happy — deep down. All is well."*

It is obvious she had said her "yes" and received a spiritual healing within. In Scripture is written this truth: **"The prayer of him that humbles himself, shall pierce the clouds, and will not depart till the Most High behold."** (Sirach 35:16 — Apocrypha)

The sincere cry of a soul to God for help and change and strength is heard above all the music of heaven and is answered. I could not give you this written testimony of His love if He had not heard and answered my prayer for help. May these written words bring you the confident assurance that you, too, WILL be changed. Expect it with child-like faith though no evidence is present as yet. Thank Him for your transformation IN ADVANCE, — believing, trusting — that it is there!

Vaya con Dios!

We'll meet on Higher Ground!

"My Lord God, I have no idea where I am going. I do not see the road ahead of me. I cannot know for certain where it will end. Nor do I really know myself, and the fact that I think I am following your will does not mean that I am actually doing so. But I believe that the desire to please you does in fact please you. And I hope I have that desire in all that I am doing. I hope that I will never do anything apart from that desire. And I know that if I do this you will lead me by the right road, though I may know nothing about it. Therefore I will trust you always though I may know nothing about it."

—Thomas Merton
Trappist Monk

Cottage, Lake Balch. Note wooden cross on front.

Higher Ground

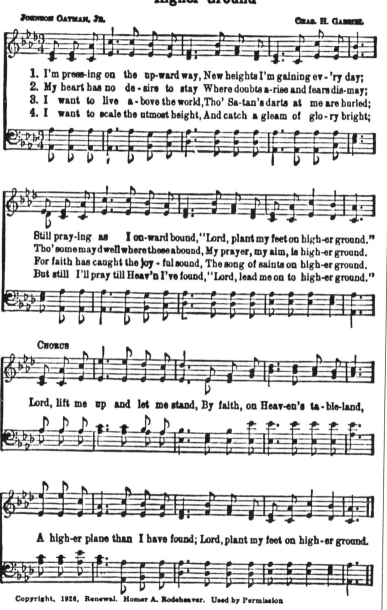

Johnson Oatman, Jr.

Chas. H. Gabriel

1. I'm press-ing on the up-ward way, New heights I'm gaining ev - 'ry day;
2. My heart has no de - sire to stay Where doubts a-rise and fears dis-may;
3. I want to live a - bove the world, Tho' Sa-tan's darts at me are hurled;
4. I want to scale the utmost height, And catch a gleam of glo - ry bright;

Still pray-ing as I on-ward bound, "Lord, plant my feet on high-er ground."
Tho' some may dwell where these abound, My prayer, my aim, is high-er ground.
For faith has caught the joy - ful sound, The song of saints on high-er ground.
But still I'll pray till Heav'n I've found, "Lord, lead me on to high-er ground."

Chorus

Lord, lift me up and let me stand, By faith, on Heav-en's ta - ble-land,

A high-er plane than I have found; Lord, plant my feet on high-er ground.